EMPLOYEE/EMPLOYER RIGHTS
A guide for the Alberta work force

Deni Cashin, LL.B.

Self-Counsel Press
(a division of)
International Self-Counsel Press Ltd.
Canada U.S.A.

Printed in Canada
First edition: August 1976
Second edition: October 1984
Third edition: July 1997

Canadian Cataloguing in Publication Data
Cashin, Deni
Employee/employer rights

(Self-counsel series)
    First ed. by Barrie Chivers and James C. Robb, with title:
    Employee/employer rights in Alberta; 2nd ed. by Timothy
    J. Christian and James C. Robb, with title: Employee/em-
    ployer rights.
ISBN 1-55180-114-0
1. Labor laws and legislation—Alberta—Popular works. I. Chivers,
Barrie. Employee/employer rights in Alberta. II. Christian, Timothy
J. Employee/employer rights. III. Title. IV. Series.
KEA400.Z82C55 1997   344.7123'01   C97-910326-6
KF3370.ZA3C55 1997

Self-Counsel Press
(a division of)
International Self-Counsel Press Ltd.

Head and Editorial Office	*U.S. Address*
1481 Charlotte Road	1704 N. State Street
North Vancouver, BC V7J 1H1	Bellingham, WA 98225

CONTENTS

NOTICE TO READERS

Laws are constantly changing. Every effort is made to keep this publication as current as possible. However, the author, the publisher, and the vendor of this book make no representation or warranties regarding the outcome or the use to which the information in this book is put and are not assuming any liability for any claims, losses, or damages arising out of the use of this book. The reader should not rely on the author or the publisher of this book for any professional advice. Please be sure that you have the most recent edition.

INTRODUCTION

The rights and obligations of employees and employers have an impact on Alberta residents in diverse ways. This book outlines the Alberta statutes, regulations, and common law (law based on court decisions made by judges) that affect the employment relationship. For some readers, this book will mark only the starting point to more indepth research in a particular area of employment law. Other readers will be satisfied with this broad-brush overview of employee/employer relations.

The ensuing discussion relates employment rights to issues of importance to people involved in both small and large business organizations. Employees, employers, human resource professionals, and small business owners all stand to benefit from a clear understanding of their rights and obligations imposed by Alberta law.

1
THE EMPLOYEE/EMPLOYER RELATIONSHIP

a. EMPLOYEE OR INDEPENDENT CONTRACTOR?

In today's employment market, important questions arise about employee rights and employer obligations and liability. The distinction between employee and independent contractor status is significant when determining employment rights and obligations. While the Employment Standards Code gives an employee basic minimum rights, the code does not apply to independent contractors. Whereas an employer is obliged to deduct employment insurance (EI), workers' compensation, Canadian Pension Plan (CPP), and income tax from an employee's wages, an employer makes no deduction from an independent contractor's wages. As well, an independent contractor is entitled to certain taxable deductions from earned income that are not available to an employee.

Sometimes it may not be clear whether a person has employee status required to assert rights under certain statutes such as the Employment Standards Code. Guidelines on how the courts approach the question of employee or independent contractor status are useful for those people with specific tax planning or liability-driven objectives.

The control test, the traditional method the courts use to determine whether an employment relationship exists, examines the degree of control exercised by the person paying for the service. A person who is told what to do and how to

1

do it is classed as an employee. A person who is free to decide how the job should be done is classed as an independent contractor. For example, A hires B to do plumbing work. A proceeds to tell B what tools to use, when to work, and how to do the plumbing job. In this situation, B is likely an employee. If B brings his or her own tools and decides when and how to do the job, B is likely an independent contractor.

In recent years, the courts have used the organization test alongside the control test. The organization test assesses the degree to which a person is part of an employer's organization. If a person is part of an employer's organization and subject to group control, the person is likely considered to be an employee.

The control test worked well in earlier times when the employer possessed the same or superior knowledge, skill, and experience as its employees. For example, the relationship between farmer and labourer is often characterized as one of employer and employee under the control test. However, in modern industrial society, the employer does not necessarily possess all the same skills as its employee. For example, a computer analyst employed by a particular company might be the only employee in the company with specialized computer skills. In light of those superior skills, the employee is not controlled by the employer in the traditional sense contemplated by the control test. However, assume that the computer analyst is paid a salary by the company on a full-time basis for an indefinite period, works for no other entity other than the company, and takes direction from the company. As the computer analyst has submitted to the employer's organizing power or power of coordination, the employee is classified as an employee using the organization test.

The courts use the following general principles as a guideline to distinguish independent contractors from employees.

(a) Is the person limited exclusively to the service of the principal?

(b) Is the person subject to control of the principal, not only as to the product or service sold, but as to when, where, and how it is sold?

(c) Does the person have an investment or interest in the tools of his or her trade or service?

(d) Has the person undertaken any personal risk in his or her own business or have any expectations of profit associated with the delivery of his or her service, as distinct from a fixed payment or commission by the principal?

(e) Is the person part of the business organization of the principal for which he or she works? In other words, whose business is it?

Each case requires careful examination. A person may characterize himself of herself as an independent contractor to take advantage of certain tax deductions. An employer may characterize a worker as an independent contractor to avoid paying social benefits, including EI, CPP, and income tax.

Despite a person's characterization for tax or other purposes, Revenue Canada or the courts may challenge the status of an independent contractor. The onus is on the individual to prove he or she is an independent contractor and not an employee. The courts tend to find employee status rather than independent contractor status. An individual who has wrongly characterized his or her employment status to Revenue Canada risks payment of all applicable taxes from the date of hiring, as well as interest and penalties.

For example, a painter submits her income tax return to Revenue Canada, indicating her status as an independent contractor. Revenue Canada examines the return and proceeds to perform an investigation of her claim. It determines that she works for only one builder and that the builder directs how and when the painting jobs should be completed. While the painter provides some of her own tools, she is not in business for herself, as she bears none of the risk of the business. Accordingly, Revenue Canada reassesses her as an employee. Certain expense deductions attributable to being self-employed are disallowed and the tax payable is recalculated. Interest is charged from the date the additional tax is owed — the filing date or April 30. As well, in some circumstances, there may be a penalty for late filing.

The employer also faces considerable risk when Revenue Canada reassesses the status of the worker from independent contractor to employee. The employer is responsible for all outstanding money owing for CPP and EI that should have been deducted during the course of the worker's employment. If the employee is still working for the employer, the employer can require the employee to pay back up to 12 months of the CPP and EI payments. However, there are limits on the amount the employer can deduct from each paycheque. If the worker no longer works for the employer, the employer is responsible for paying the whole amount. In that case, the employer has no recourse against the employee for reimbursement since deductions for EI and CPP are the employer's responsibility. The employer also faces a penalty for failure to deduct, in addition to repayment of money owing for unpaid deductions.

If an employer or worker has questions about the status of a worker as independent contractor or as employee, a ruling in writing can be requested from Revenue Canada. To expedite the request, an employer can request a CPT 1 Form and an employee can request a CPT 2 Form from the Forms office:

Forms Office
Revenue Canada
EI and CPP Ruling Department
220 - 4th Avenue S.E.
Calgary, AB T2G 0L1
Tel: (403) 221-8900 to obtain form
Tel: (403) 221-8970 for inquires

b. BENEFITS OF AN EMPLOYMENT CONTRACT TO AN EMPLOYEE

An employment contract allows the employee to bargain for better terms than the minimum standard the law provides. As well, employment contracts help employees understand their rights at the time employment is offered. Even if the majority of employees find the terms offered in an employment contract difficult or impossible to negotiate, at least they know exactly where they stand. For example, there may be some advantage to an employee knowing that six months' wages will be paid if he or she is dismissed without cause. While the entitlement under common law may be higher, the employee has no certainty of winning a wrongful dismissal case in court. As well, legal costs to enforce rights could prove prohibitive. Employment contracts are desirable for employees at all levels, not just senior-level employees.

Suggested terms for an employment contract drawn from an employee's perspective include the following:

(a) salary and method of payment;

(b) salary reviews and increases;

(c) medical and insurance benefits, vacations, car allowances, stock options;

(d) relocation requirements and relocation benefits;

(e) definition of job duties and responsibilities;

(f) description of all company policies, rules, and procedures;

(g) provision to ensure that incentive compensation is tied to a formula, as opposed to being discretionary on the part of the employer;

(h) severance pay to be paid on dismissal without cause;

(i) treatment of company property, confidentiality, and non-disclosure agreements; and

(j) provision of relocation counselling and other job replacement support.

If an employee is asked to sign an employment contract containing restrictions on employment with a competitor or setting up a similar business, he or she should ensure that those restrictions are not excessive. A restriction on an employee setting up a similar business within a reasonable geographical area after a reasonable length of time has passed after the employment has ended would not be considered excessive.

c. BENEFITS OF AN EMPLOYMENT CONTRACT TO AN EMPLOYER

An employment contract allows the employer an opportunity to exercise more control over the employee/employer relationship. For example an employer can describe in the employment contract the type of conduct that will justify immediate dismissal for cause. The employer can state that job transfers or changes in job responsibilities will not constitute constructive dismissal or wrongful dismissal. An employer can set out the amount of payment the employee will receive if he or she is dismissed without cause. While the payment amount cannot be less than that required under the Employment Standards Code, it may be less than the amount that might have been awarded in a court case.

Suggested terms for an employment contract drawn from an employer's perspective include the following:

(a) flexible definition of duties and responsibilities;

(b) waiver of commitment to a fixed or definite support staff;

(c) requirement to relocate;

(d) power to reduce salary in certain circumstances;

(e) description of what is considered dismissal with just cause;

(f) notice to be provided on dismissal without cause;

(g) restrictions on employment with a competitor or setting up a similar business after termination of employment;

(h) non-disclosure and confidentiality agreement for trade secrets and customer lists;

(i) nature and payment of relocation counselling services to be provided;

(j) no guarantee of annual salary increments;

(k) salary, benefits, incentive compensation, pension, deferred profit-sharing plan, allowable business expenses, policy about illness or other absence; and

(l) a probationary period.

2
EMPLOYMENT STANDARDS

a. THE EMPLOYMENT STANDARDS CODE

The Employment Standards Code establishes minimum standards of conditions of employment for employees, including minimum wage, maximum hours of work, overtime rate, statutory holidays, vacation, maternity or adoption leave, and minimum severance pay on dismissal. Many workers in Alberta have little control over terms of their employment. While chapter 1 discusses employment contracts and those clauses advantageous to both employees and employers, most of us are not in a position to seriously challenge terms of employment offered by prospective employers. Workers with limited bargaining power benefit from understanding the minimum rights granted under the code. Similarly, employers can make better business decisions once their minimum obligations are understood.

The Employment Standards Code sets out the minimum rights and obligations of employers and employees in Alberta. The new code came into effect on March 1, 1997. Its focus is to simplify and clarify wording in the old code. For the most part, substantive rights and responsibilities of employees and employers under the code have not changed.

b. APPLICATION OF THE CODE

1. Whom does the code protect?

The code applies to all employees and employers in Alberta. People exempt from certain parts of the code are discussed below, in section **b.2.**, as well in the discussions of the specific provisions that follow.

(a) People covered by the Public Service Employee Relations Act and the Police Act

The new code applies to employers and employees covered by the Public Service Employee Relations Act. Employers and employees regulated by the Police Act are bound only to those provisions for maternity and adoption benefits.

Certain employees and employers are exempt from the code or parts of the code if another statute states that the code does not apply.

(b) Farm labourers

Workers employed on a farm or ranch whose employment is directly related to the primary production of eggs, milk, grain, seeds, fruit, vegetables, honey, livestock, game-production animals, poultry, or bees are exempt from provisions for hours of work and overtime pay, minimum wage, vacations and vacation pay, general holidays and general holiday pay, and employment of young people.

(c) Domestic workers

Employees employed in domestic work in a private dwelling are exempted from the provisions for minimum wage, general holidays and general holiday pay, hours of work and overtime pay, and notice about work schedules.

Domestic workers are entitled to their agreed wages (which can be below minimum wage), vacations and vacation pay, notice of termination of employment, parental benefits, and days of rest as stipulated by the code.

(d) Federal employees

Employees regulated by federal legislation — the Canada Labour Code — are not covered by the Alberta Employment Standards Code. Federally regulated industries include navigation and shipping, railway, airlines, broadcasting, and banking.

2. Right to pursue civil remedies

Nothing in the code affects any civil remedy that an employee has against his or her employer or that an employer has against its employee. For example, if an employee has been wrongfully dismissed by his or her employer, the employee may submit a claim under the code for unpaid holiday pay, overtime pay, or wages due on termination of employment. Alternatively, the employee may choose to pursue common law rights and bring an action in the appropriate court for damages caused by the wrongful dismissal.

3. Minimum standards cannot be avoided

An agreement between an employee and his or her employer that the code or a provision of it does not apply or that the remedies the code provides are not to be available to one or both of the party's benefit is prohibited. For example, a verbal or written agreement to a term that the employee is to receive a set wage with no holiday pay is prohibited by the code.

4. Greater benefits in employment contract prevail

If the employee and employer have an agreement that gives the employee greater rights than those the code provides in terms of wages; overtime pay; maternity, adoption, or parental benefits; or any other benefits, that agreement prevails over the minimum standards in the code.

For example, if an employee's employment contract provides for a paid 20-week maternity leave, that contract provision overrides the minimum standard of an unpaid 18-week maternity leave employees on the job at least one year are entitled to under the code. Similarly, if the employer has agreed to greater obligations or duties than the code requires, the agreement overrides the code.

5. Continuous employment

Employment of employees is considered continuous for the purposes of the code when a business is sold, leased, transferred, or merged, or when it continues to operate under a receiver-manager. For example, consider a long-time employee who is dismissed several months after the original employer sells the business to new owners. To calculate termination pay, length of employment will be calculated from the date the employee began employment with the original employer.

6. Penalties for non-compliance with code

An employer, employee, director, officer, or other person who is guilty of an offence under the code is liable to pay a fine. The fines are —

(a) if a corporation, not more than $100 000; or

(b) if an individual, not more than $50 000.

Prosecution for an offence under the code must begin within one year from the date the alleged offence occurred.

If a corporation commits an offence under the code, every director or officer who directed, authorized, assented to, permitted, participated in, or acquiesced in the offence is guilty of the offence, whether or not the corporation has been prosecuted or convicted.

c. EMPLOYMENT RECORDS

Every employer must maintain an up-to-date record of employment for each employee except those listed, in section c.2 below.

1. What records must be kept?

The record of employment must contain particulars, including:

(a) regular and overtime hours of work;

(b) wage rate and overtime rate;

(c) earnings paid, showing separately each component of the earnings for each pay period;

(d) deductions from earnings and the reason for each deduction;

(e) time off instead of overtime pay provided and taken;

(f) name, address, and date of birth of employee;

(g) the date the present period of employment started;

(h) the date on which a general holiday is taken;

(i) each annual vacation, showing the date it started and finished and the period of employment in which the annual vacation was earned;

(j) the wage rate and overtime rate when employment starts, the date of any change to wage rates or overtime rates, and particulars of every change to them;

(k) copies of documentation of maternity and adoption benefits; and

(l) copies of any termination notice and of written requests to employees to return to work after a temporary layoff.

The employer must retain employment records for at least three years from the date the record is made.

At the end of each pay period, the employer must give employees a detailed statement of employment showing:

(a) regular hours of work,

(b) overtime hours of work,

(c) wage rate and overtime rate,

(d) earnings paid, showing separately each component of the earnings for each pay period,

(e) deductions from earnings and the reason for each deduction,

(f) time off instead of overtime pay provided and taken, and

(g) period of employment the statement covers.

The hours of work of an employee must be recorded daily. On request, the employer must provide the employee with a detailed statement of how the employee's earnings were calculated and the method of calculating any bonus or living allowance paid, whether or not it forms part of wages.

It is an offence for an employer to falsify employment records or to fail to retain employment records.

2. Exemptions

Employees, and their employers, who are exempt from the sections of the code dealing with employment records are the same as those exempt from the sections dealing with hours of work and overtime pay, namely.

- Salespeople, other than route salespeople, paid whole or in part by commission, who solicit orders, principally outside the place of business of their employers, for goods or services or both that will be delivered or provided to the purchasers

- Automobile, recreational vehicle, truck, or bus salespeople

- Mobile home salespeople

- Farm machinery salespeople

- Heavy-duty construction equipment or road construction equipment salespeople

- Residential home salespeople who are not real estate agents licensed under the Real Estate Agent's Licensing Act

- Real estate agents licensed under the Real Estate Agents' Licensing Act, or salespeople of those agents

- Salespeople registered under the Securities Act

- Registered architects
- Lawyers or students articled to lawyers
- Chartered accountants or students articled to chartered accountants
- Certified general accountants (CGAs) or students articled to CGAs
- Certified management accountants
- Registered chiropractors
- Registered dental professionals
- Professional engineers, geologists, and geophysicists
- Optometrists
- Podiatrists
- Chartered psychologists
- Individuals holding a certificate under section 512 of the Insurance Act
- Salespeople for direct sellers licensed under the Licensing of Trades and Businesses Act
- Land agents licensed under the Land Agents Licensing Act
- Extras in film or video production

d. PAYMENT OF EARNINGS

1. Pay periods

Every employer must establish one or more pay periods for the calculation of wages and overtime pay due to an employee. A pay period must not be longer than one "work month," which is defined as a calendar month or the period from a time on a specific day in a month to the same time on the same day in the following month as established by the consistent practice of an employer.

2. Timing for payment of wages, overtime pay, and holiday pay

The employer must pay wages, overtime pay, and entitlements the employee has earned within ten days after the end of each pay period. When employment is terminated on notice by the employer or the employee, or when the employer pays termination pay in lieu of notice, the employer must pay earnings no later than three consecutive days after the last day of employment.

When an employee is required to give termination notice but quits without doing so, the employer must pay the employee's earnings not later than ten consecutive days after the date on which the notice would have expired if it had been given.

An employer must give notice of any deduction in wages.

3. Deductions from earnings

With few exceptions, the employer may not make any deductions from wages, overtime pay, or other employee entitlements. An employer may make deductions only when:

(a) another act, regulation, or order of the court requires it;

(b) the employee has personally authorized in writing the deduction; or

(c) it is authorized by a collective agreement.

Required and permitted deductions are employee contributions to CPP and EI, Alberta Health Care premiums, and garnishees.

Despite written authorization from an employee or an authorization in a collective agreement, an employer is never permitted to deduct amounts from earnings because of faulty work or cash shortages or loss of property, if someone other than that employee has access to the cash or property.

Where deductions are permitted, the employer must notify the employee of the deduction before the beginning of the pay period in which the deduction is to take place. If an employer fails to give this notice, an employee is entitled to the difference between the employee's wage rate, overtime rate, vacation pay, general holiday pay, or termination pay before the deduction and those rates and pay after the deduction, from the time in the pay period in which the deduction was first applied to the end of that pay period.

Both the employer and the employee are in violation of the code if the employee, directly or indirectly (e.g., by absorbing the cost of an employer's expense), returns money to the employer, effecting a reduction of wages in violation of the code. For example, the code prohibits any reduction that brings the employee's wage to under minimum wage.

4. Garnishment of wages

An employer may not dismiss, lay off, or suspend an employee because garnishment proceedings are being taken against that employee. Garnishment occurs when the employer is required by a court order or garnishment to pay a portion of the employee's wages to a third party.

e. MINIMUM WAGE

1. Minimum hourly rate

Minimum wage for all employees other than those people listed below and those excluded from minimum wage requirements (see section **e.2.** below) is $5.00 an hour. (**Note:** Minimum wage is subject to change. Please check with the Employment Standards Branch for any update to wage rates.) Those people subject to a different minimum wage are listed below.

    (a) students under 18 years of age employed after school or on weekends or holidays must be paid at least $4.50 an hour;

(b) a minimum wage of $200.00 a week is payable to —

  (i) Salespeople for commercial agents licensed under the Licensing of Trades and Businesses Act

  (ii) Salespeople, other than route salespeople, paid in whole or in part by commission, who solicit orders mainly outside the office for goods or services or both, which will subsequently be provided to the purchasers

  (iii) Automobile, truck, or bus salespeople

  (iv) Mobile home salespeople

  (v) Farm machinery salespeople

  (vi) Heavy-duty construction equipment or road construction equipment salespeople

  (vii) Residential home salespeople who are not licensed under the Real Estate Agents' Licensing Act.

Both the employee and the employer are in violation of the code if the employee works for less than the minimum wage.

2. **Exemptions**

Certain employees are exempt from the minimum wage requirements. These include:

- Lawyers or individuals articled to lawyers

- Chartered accountants or individuals articled to chartered accountants

- Real estate agents licensed under the Real Estate Agents' Licensing Act or salespeople of those agents

- Salespeople registered under the Securities Act

- Individuals holding a certificate under section 512 of the Insurance Act

17

- Land agents licensed under the Land Agents Licensing Act

- Students engaged in a work experience program or formal course of training under the Minister of Education

- Extras in film or video production

- Farm labourers (see section **b.1.**)

- Domestic workers (see section **b.1.**)

3. **Minimum wage for employees with restricted hours of work**

Employees working for less than two consecutive hours of work for a non-profit recreation centre or athletic centre owned by the city, school bus drivers, and students under 18 years of age working outside school hours must be paid for two hours of work at the minimum wage.

Employees other than those listed in the paragraph above, who are employed for less than three hours must be paid for three hours of work at minimum wage. A meal period of one hour or less is not considered part of the three hours; hours before the meal and after the meal are considered consecutive.

4. **Deductions from minimum wage**

Deductions from minimum wage for board and lodging must not exceed $1.65 for a single meal and $2.20 a day for lodging. No deduction is permitted for meals the employee does not consume. No deduction from minimum wage can be made for use, repair, or laundering of uniforms or other special articles of clothing required for work.

5. **People with handicaps**

The director may issue to the employer of an person who is handicapped a permit authorizing the employer to pay that person a wage at less than the applicable minimum wage.

The director issues such a permit only when he or she is satisfied that the employment arrangement between the employer and employee is satisfactory for both parties in all the circumstances.

f. HOURS OF WORK AND OVERTIME PAY

1. Overtime rates

An employer cannot require or permit an employee to work more than 8 hours in a day or 44 hours in a week unless the employer pays the employee an overtime rate of 1.5 times the wages of the employee. As discussed below, exceptions are made for employees who are subject to collective agreements, employment contracts, compressed work weeks, and specific exemptions.

If an employee works less than 44 hours in a week but works more than 8 hours in a given day, the employee must be paid overtime rate of 1.5 times his or her wages for those hours per day that exceed 8 hours.

If an employee works more than 44 hours in the week and more than 8 hours in any day, calculation of overtime must be made on the basis of that number of hours each day over 8 hours and the number of hours exceeding 44. Overtime must be paid according to whichever method of calculation results in greater pay.

Both the employer and the employee are in violation of the code if the employee works for less than the overtime rate to which he or she is entitled.

Overtime hours are modified by regulation for certain industries, including —

- Ambulance driving and attending
- Trucking
- Oil-well servicing
- Highway and railway construction

- Brush clearing
- Field services (including road construction, maintenance, and snow removal by municipal district or counties; and geophysical exploration, logging, and lumbering in certain circumstances)
- Nurseries (i.e., the gardening industry, including preparation of tress, shrubs, and plants for sale)
- Irrigation
- Taxicab services

2. Time off in lieu of overtime

Employees and employers may agree in their collective agreements or written employment contracts that the employees will take time off with pay instead of overtime pay. Unless provided otherwise in a collective agreement or a certificate from the director of employment standards, time off with pay must be provided and paid within three months of the end of the pay period in which it was earned. An employer must provide a copy of the overtime agreement to each employee affected by it.

3. Calculation of overtime rate for employees paid commission

If an employee is paid partly by salary and partly by commission, to calculate overtime pay the employee's wage rate is based on the salary component of the wages so long as that component is greater than the minimum wage. If the salary component is less than the minimum wage, the employee's wage rate is considered the minimum wage, and the overtime rate will be calculated on the minimum wage rate.

If an employee is paid entirely on commission or other incentive-based remuneration, to calculate overtime pay the employee's wage rate is considered the minimum wage. Again, the overtime rate will be calculated on the minimum wage rate.

4. Compressed work week

An employer may require or permit an employee to work a compressed work week, a week consisting of fewer work days in the work week and more hours of work in a work day, paid at the employee's regular wage rate. However, a compressed work week must be scheduled in advance and the schedule must meet the following requirements:

(a) if the compressed work week is part of a cycle, the schedule must show all the work weeks that make up the cycle;

(b) the maximum hours of work that an employee may be scheduled to work in a work day is 12;

(c) the maximum hours of work that an employee may be scheduled to work in a compressed work week is 44; and

(d) if the compressed work week is part of a cycle, the maximum average weekly hours of work that an employee may be scheduled to work in the cycle is 44.

5. Exemptions

The Exemption Regulation under the code exempts certain employees from parts of the code. Employees and their employers who are exempt under the sections of the code dealing with hours of work, overtime pay, and employment records include:

- Salespeople, other than route salespeople, paid whole or in part by commission, who solicit orders, principally outside the place of business of their employers, for goods or services or both that will be delivered or provided to the purchasers

- Automobile, recreational vehicle, truck, or bus salespeople

- Mobile home salespeople

21

- Farm machinery salespeople
- Heavy-duty construction equipment or road construction equipment salespeople
- Residential home salespeople who are not real estate agents licensed under the Real Estate Agents' Licensing Act
- Real estate agents licensed under the Real Estate Agents' Licensing Act, or salespeople of those agents
- Salespeople registered under the Securities Act
- Individuals holding a certificate under section 512 of the Insurance Act
- Salespeople for direct sellers licensed under the Licensing of Trades and Businesses Act
- Land agents licensed under the Land Agents Licensing Act
- Extras in film or video production
- Farm labourers (see section **b.1.**)
- Domestic workers (see section **b.1.**)
- Registered architects
- Lawyers or students articled to lawyers
- Chartered accountants or students articled to chartered accountants
- Certified general accountants (CGAs) or students articled to CGAs
- Certified management accountants
- Registered chiropractors
- Registered dental professionals
- Professional engineers, geologists, and geophysicists
- Optometrists

- Podiatrists

- Chartered psychologists

As well, an employer is not required to pay overtime rates to supervisors, managers, or an employee who deals with confidential matters, (i.e., employees who have access to information not available to the majority of employees). For example, a highly paid senior executive would not be entitled to earn overtime pay.

An officer from the Employment Standards Branch is authorized to decide whether a person is an exempted employee. An employer or employee affected by the officer's decision may appeal the umpire's decision (see section **m.** below for more on appeals).

6. **Maximum daily hours of work**

An employer cannot require employees to work more than 12 consecutive hours in any one day unless:

   (a) an accident occurs, urgent work is necessary, or other unforeseeable or unpreventable circumstances occur; or

   (b) an employer obtains a permit from an employment standards director authorizing extended hours.

If hours of work must be extended, they should increase only to the extent necessary to avoid serious interference with the ordinary working of the business.

7. **Hours of rest**

An employer must give an employee at least:

   (a) 1 day of rest each week,

   (b) 2 consecutive days of rest after 2 consecutive weeks of work,

   (c) 3 consecutive days of rest after 3 consecutive weeks of work, and

23

(d) 4 consecutive days of rest after 4 consecutive weeks of work.

As well, an employer must give an employee 4 consecutive days of rest after working for more than 24 consecutive days.

An employer must give an employee a paid or unpaid rest period of at least one-half hour during each work shift longer than 5 consecutive hours unless:

(a) an accident occurs, urgent work is necessary, or other unforeseeable or unpreventable circumstances occur;

(b) a collective agreement provides otherwise; or

(c) it is not reasonable for the employee to take a rest period.

Employers must post notices in visible places notifying employees when work or shifts begin and end. An employee is not required to change from one shift to another shift without at least 24 hours of notice in writing of the change in shift and 8 hours of rest between shifts.

Section 5. above lists those workers who are exempt from this provision of the code.

8. Sick leave

There is no provincial legislation in Alberta dealing with sick leave. The employer must pay only for hours worked. Sick leave policies are at the discretion of the employer.

g. ANNUAL VACATIONS

1. When is an employee eligible?

After each year of employment, an employee must receive at least two weeks of annual vacation with vacation pay. After five years of employment with the same employer, an employee is entitled to at least three weeks of annual vacation with vacation pay.

If an employee does not work for his or her employer for all the days that employee was normally scheduled to work, the employer may reduce the employee's vacation and vacation pay proportionately.

The employer may establish a common anniversary date for calculating vacation and vacation pay, but it must not result in a reduction to those entitlements for any employee.

The employer must give the annual vacation in one unbroken period, unless the employee requests otherwise in writing. Despite any employee request, a vacation period must be taken in periods of not less than one day.

2. Vacation pay

Vacation pay for each week of vacation for an employee who is paid monthly is the wage of the employee for his or her normal hours of work in a month divided by four and one third. For example, if an employee is paid $1 200 per month, the vacation pay is $1 200 divided by 4⅓, or $276.92, payable for each week of vacation the employee is entitled to.

Vacation pay of an employee who has been employed less than five years is 4% of the employee's gross earnings and 6% if the employee has been employed more than five years.

3. Payment

An employer may pay vacation pay at any time before an employee's annual vacation, but *must* pay vacation pay to each employee no later than the next regularly scheduled payday after the employee starts annual vacation. If vacation pay has not been fully paid before the annual vacation starts, the employee may request the employer pay vacation pay at least one day before the vacation starts. The employer must comply with this request.

If an employee quits before taking an annual vacation, the employer must pay to that employee the vacation pay the employee was entitled to for that year, plus a percentage of the wages for the period since the date the employee was last entitled to annual vacation. This must be paid as soon as possible after the employment ends.

The construction industry has different rules under the code.

4. Exemptions

The sections pertaining to vacation and vacation pay do not apply to:

- Salespeople, other than route salespeople, remunerated in whole or part by commission, who solicit orders, principally outside the place of business of their employers, for goods or services or both, which will be delivered or provided to the purchasers

- Real estate agents licensed under the Real Estate Agents' Licensing Act or salespeople of those agents

- Salespeople registered under the Securities Act

- Individuals holding a certificate under section 512 of the Insurance Act

- Extras in film or video production

- Farm labourers (see section **b.1.**)

h. GENERAL HOLIDAYS AND GENERAL HOLIDAY PAY

General holidays in Alberta are:

(a) New Year's Day

(b) Alberta Family Day

(c) Good Friday

(d) Victoria Day

(e) Canada Day

26

(f) Labour Day

(g) Thanksgiving Day

(h) Remembrance Day

(i) Christmas Day

1. Employee with regular work schedules

An employee is entitled to general holiday pay unless the employee:

(a) has worked for less than 30 days during the preceding 12 months;

(b) does not work on a general holiday when he or she is required or scheduled to do so; or

(c) is absent from employment without consent the last day before or the first day after a general holiday.

(a) General holiday falling on regular working day

If the general holiday falls on an employee's regular working day, the employee must receive general holiday pay at least equal to his or her daily wage.

If the employee works on a general holiday, the employee must receive the greater of either 1.5 times the hourly wage for the hours worked or the amount equal to his or her daily wage. Alternatively, the employer can pay the employee the regular daily wage and give the employee one day holiday, to be taken not later than the next annual vacation of the employee.

(b) General holiday falling on day that is not a regular working day

If an employee is required to work on a general holiday that is not a regular working day, the employer must pay 1.5 times the hourly wage for the hours worked on that day.

(c) General holiday falling within employee's annual vacation

If a general holiday falls within an employee's annual vacation, the employer must give the employee an extra day of holiday on what would have been the employee's first day back or another day by mutual agreement between the employee and employer. In these circumstances, the general holiday pay must be at least equal to the employee's average daily wage.

2. Employee working irregular schedules

When an employee works an irregular schedule, there is sometimes doubt about whether a general holiday is on a day that would normally have been a work day for the employee. If in at least five of the nine weeks preceding the work week in which the general holiday occurs, the employee worked on the same day of the week as the day on which the general holiday falls, the general holiday is considered a day that would have been a work day for the employee.

3. Employee paid by commission

If an employee is paid entirely by commission or other incentive-based remuneration, to calculate general holiday pay, the employee's wage rate is considered the minimum wage. For example, suppose a salesperson is paid entirely by commission. Her holiday pay is calculated using the minimum wage rate multiplied by the number of hours she works in a day.

If an employee is paid partly by salary and partly by commission, then, to calculate general holiday pay, the employee's wage rate is based on the salary component of the wages so long as the salary component is greater than the minimum wage.

If the salary component is less than the minimum wage, the employee's wage rate is considered the minimum wage. For example, if a salesperson is paid $100 per week in salary plus commissions, general holiday pay is also calculated as minimum wage multiplied by the number of hours a day, since the salary component of the income is below the minimum wage.

4. Exemptions

The sections of the codes pertaining to general holidays and general holiday pay do not apply to:

- Salespeople, other than route salespeople, remunerated in whole or part by commission, who solicit orders, principally outside the place of business of their employers, for goods or services or both, which will be delivered or provided to the purchasers

- Automobile, recreational vehicle, truck, or bus salespeople

- Mobile home salespeople

- Farm machinery salespeople

- Heavy-duty construction equipment or road construction equipment salespeople

- Real estate agents licensed under the Real Estate Agents' Licensing Act or salespeople of those agents

- Salespeople registered under the Securities Act

- Individuals holding a certificate under section 512 of the Insurance Act

- Extras in film or video production

- Farm labourers (see section **b.1.**)

- Domestic workers (see section **b.1.**)

i. TERMINATION OF EMPLOYMENT

1. Reasonable notice to employee

No employee may be dismissed without notice of termination or payment of a sum of money (in an amount specified by the code) instead of notice, *or* a combination of both notice and monetary compensation, except in the circumstances listed below in section 3.

2. Minimum notice to employee

An employee must receive written notice of termination of employment, or payment at least equal to the wages the employee would have earned during the period of reasonable notice, as follows:

(a) one week, if length of employment is more than three months and less than two years;

(b) two weeks, if length of employment is more than two years and less than four years;

(c) four weeks, if length of employment is more than four years and less than six years;

(d) five weeks, if length of employment is more than six years but less than eight years; and

(e) eight weeks, if length of employment is ten years or more.

An employer may dismiss an employee by using a combination of notice and termination pay in lieu of notice. If money is paid in lieu of notice, the employee is entitled to be paid immediately after being dismissed.

3. When is reasonable notice to employee not required?

Reasonable notice (or termination pay in lieu of notice) to an employee is not required when:

(a) the employee has been employed by the employer for three months or less;

(b) the employee is dismissed for cause, (i.e., the employee has violated terms of the employment relationship. See chapter 3 for a discussion of dismissal with cause);

(c) the employee is temporarily laid off (a layoff of less than 60 days or a layoff of more than 60 days during which time the employee is receiving an agreed-on amount of money or benefits from the employer);

(d) the employee is laid off after refusing an employer's offer of reasonable alternative work;

(e) the employee refuses work made available through a seniority system;

(f) the employee is not working because of a strike or lockout at the workplace;

(g) the employee on temporary layoff does not return to work within seven days after being asked to do so in writing by the employer;

(h) the employee is employed under an agreement by which the employee may elect either to work or not work for a temporary period when asked to do so by the employer;

(i) the contract of employment is or has become impossible for the employer to perform because of unforeseeable or unpreventable causes beyond the control of the employer; or

(j) the employee is employed on a seasonal basis and his or her employment ends at the end of the season.

Special provisions apply to workers in construction, erection, repair and interior decoration of buildings, roads, sidewalks, pipelines, irrigation systems, earth and rock dams, sewage, power transmission and distribution systems, and cutting and disposing of bush and trees. The code and regulations details these particulars.

4. Reasonable notice to employer

The code also requires an employee to give the employer reasonable notice of his or her quitting. However, this section of the code is usually not enforced. If an employee has been employed by the employer for more than three weeks but less than two years, one week of notice should be given. Two weeks of notice is required for a length of employment greater than two years.

An employee is not required to give notice if:

(a) the established custom in the industry is to give no notice;

(b) the employee quits because continued employment poses danger to his or her health or safety;

(c) the contract of employment cannot be performed because of unforeseeable or unpreventable causes; or

(d) the employee quits because of a reduction in wage rate, overtime rate, or entitlements.

5. Wrongful dismissal

The code sets out the minimum notice required for an employee based on his or her length of employment. The termination payment the code requires is separate from any remedy that may be available to an employee through the courts.

For example, suppose a woman is fired without cause from her managerial position after one year of employment. Under the code, she is entitled to a minimum of one week of notice. If the woman is not given notice and is asked to leave immediately, she must be paid at least one week's salary. However, if the woman was lured away from a senior position to work for the employer, if the industry she is working in has a narrow niche with few job openings, and if the woman is 55 years old and has restricted opportunities because of her age, her remedy through the courts may be considerably greater than one week's salary. Chapter 3 discusses in more detail wrongful dismissal and remedies available through the courts.

j. LAYOFF AND RECALL

If an employer wishes to maintain an employment relationship without terminating the employment of an employee, the employer may temporarily lay off the employee. On the 60th consecutive day of temporary layoff, an employee's employment ends and the employer must pay the employee termination pay unless:

(a) after the layoff starts, and by agreement between the employer and employee, an employer pays the employee wages or an amount instead of wages, in which case the employment ends and termination pay is payable when the agreement ends;

(b) the employer makes payments for the benefit of the laid-off employee under a pension or employee insurance plan or the like, in which case employment ends and termination pay is payable when the payments cease; or

(c) there is a collective agreement binding the employer and employee containing recall rights for employees following layoff, in which case employment ends and termination pay is payable when the recall rights expire.

If an employee fails to return to work within seven consecutive days after being requested to do so in writing by the employer, the employee is not entitled to termination notice or termination pay. This rule does not apply if the employee is bound by a collective agreement containing recall rights for employees following a layoff.

k. PARENTAL BENEFITS

1. Maternity leave

A pregnant employee is entitled to 18 weeks of maternity leave without pay so long as she has been employed by an employer continuously for one year. The leave cannot exceed 18 weeks and may begin any time within 12 weeks before the expected date of delivery. The 18 weeks is extended by the number of days between the due date and the actual delivery date, if not the same.

If the pregnant employee has worked less than one year for the employer, she is entitled to a maternity leave under the Human Rights, Citizenship and Multiculturalism Act. The woman's doctor determines the length of the maternity leave. The doctor provides a medical certificate stating the time the woman needs to recover from the pregnancy before returning to work. Doctor-prescribed maternity leaves vary in length from 2 to 16 weeks.

The maternity leave must include six weeks following the birth of the baby, unless the employee and employer agree to shorten the leave. If they agree that the employee will return to work earlier than six weeks following the birth, the employee must obtain a medical certificate from her doctor indicating that her health will not be injured by resuming work.

Before beginning maternity leave, the employee must give the employer at least two weeks of notice in writing of the day on which she intends to begin maternity leave. If asked by her employer, the employee must also provide a medical certificate certifying that she is pregnant and giving the estimated date of delivery.

If the employee fails to give two weeks of notice before beginning maternity leave, she may, within two weeks of stopping work, provide the employer with a medical certificate indicating that she is not able to work because of a medical condition arising from her pregnancy. The certificate should also state the estimated date of delivery or actual date of delivery.

See chapter 4 for more discussion of this issue.

The code offers no parental leave rights to fathers.

2. Extended maternity leave

If an employee is unable to return to work after her maternity leave because of a medical condition of her or her child, the employer must grant her an extended leave of up to three weeks, so long as the employee provides a medical certificate indicating that she is unable to work because of a medical condition following delivery.

3. Notice by employer to begin maternity leave

If the employee is unable to perform her duties of employment during the 12 weeks before her delivery date, the employer may, by notice in writing, require the employee to take her leave.

4. Adoption leave

An employer must grant adoption leave to an employee adopting a child under the age of three years if the employee has been working for the employer for at least one year. The employee must submit a written notice of leave to the employer at least two weeks before the employee reasonably expects to first obtain custody of the child. Failing two weeks of notice, the employee must give notice to the employer immediately after receiving notice of the adoption.

Adoption leave is not more than eight weeks, without pay, beginning on the date the adoptive parent first obtains custody of the adopted child. Only one parent of a child can be granted adoption leave.

5. Rules common to maternity and adoption

An employer cannot fire or lay off an employee who is on maternity leave or who is entitled to or who is on adoption leave.

The employee must give the employer two weeks of notice of when he or she intends to resume work. The employer must reinstate the employee in the position he or she had at the time the leave began, or provide the employee with comparable work. Wages, entitlements, and other benefits accruing in the employee's position after leave began must be the same as that before the leave began.

An employee who does not wish to resume employment after maternity or adoption leave must give the employer two weeks of notice of his or her intent to quit.

If an employer has suspended or discontinued the business entirely or partly during an employee's maternity or adoption leave, on resumption of the business, the employer must reinstate the employee in the same or equivalent position, with the same wages the employee had before the leave. Alternatively, the employer must provide the employee with work, following an established seniority system in force at the time the employee's leave began. The employer is obligated for one year from the last day of the employee's maternity or adoption leave to reinstate that employee.

l. EMPLOYMENT OF YOUNG PEOPLE

A person who must attend school under the School Act is prohibited from working during regular school hours. Also, no person younger than 15 years old can be employed without the written consent of his or her parent or guardian and the approval of the director of Employment Standards. Exceptions to these two rules are made only for those people who have received special approval under the School Act to pursue vocational training or participate in a work-experience program.

So long as the work is not injurious to his or her life, health, education, or welfare, an adolescent (person under 15 years but 12 years or older) may be employed as a:

(a) delivery person of small wares for a retail store,

(b) clerk or messenger in an office,

(c) clerk in a retail store, or

(d) delivery person distributing newspapers, flyers, or handbills.

However, an adolescent may not work more than two hours on a school day or more than eight hours during a non-school day. An adolescent also may not work 9:00 p.m. through to 6:00 a.m.

A "young" person (15 years or older but younger than 18 years) may not work between 9:00 p.m. and 12:01 a.m. in certain businesses if not in the continuous presence of a least one other person 18 years or older. This restriction applies to retail businesses selling food, beverages (alcoholic or not), or gasoline, or an establishment such as a hotel or motel where a licence is required under the Licensing of Trades and Businesses Act.

As well, "young" people may not work in these businesses between 12:01 a.m. and 6:00 a.m. Businesses not specified in the regulations may hire "young" people between 12:01 a.m. and 6:00 a.m. so long as the parent or guardian has given written consent and the "young" person works in the continuous presence of a person 18 years or older.

Farm labourers are exempt from this provision of the code. See section **b.1.** earlier in this chapter for further details.

m. THE COMPLAINT PROCESS

1. Complaint to officer

An employer may not discharge, restrict the employment of, or discriminate against an employee for making a complaint under the Employment Standards Code, giving evidence under the code, or making any disclosures as the code requires.

An employee may make a written complaint to an employment standards officer that he or she:

(a) is entitled to but did not receive wages, overtime pay, entitlements, notice regarding reduction in wages, or parental benefits;

(b) was dismissed, fired, laid off, or suspended for the sole reason that garnishment proceedings are being or may be taken against him or her;

(c) was discharged, restricted, or in any way discriminated against because that employee —

(i) has made a complaint under the code,

(ii) has given evidence or may give evidence at any inquiry or in any proceeding or prosecution under the code,

(iii) requests or demands anything to which he or she is entitled to under the code, or

(iv) has made or is about to make any statement or disclosure that may be required of him or her under the code.

There is no fee for the employee to make a complaint or for the investigation of a complaint.

It is an offence to give false information or to make an untrue complaint to an officer.

Complaints must be made within six months if the employee is fired or quits. The director may extend the six-month limit if there are extenuating circumstances.

An officer may attempt to mediate or settle the differences between the employer and the employee. If an officer is unable to bring about a settlement in the instances listed above, the officer must refer the complaint to the director. In instances other than those listed above, the officer may order the employer to pay the employee money owing for wages or other entitlements or to compensate the employee for money deducted from wages in violation of the code.

An officer may refuse to investigate a complaint if it is frivolous, if there is insufficient evidence, or if the employee is pursuing the same complaint in a court or other tribunal. If an officer refuses to investigate a complaint, the employee may appeal the officer's decision within 21 days by notifying the director in writing of his or her appeal and specifying the reasons for the appeal.

2. Authority of officers

When investigating a complaint, an officer may —

(a) enter at any reasonable time any premises in which the officer has reason to believe that an individual is or was employed, to inspect the employment records and make copies of them;

(b) require an employer, employee, or any other person to provide oral or written statements about any matter relating to employment or employment records;

(c) make any inspection, investigation, and inquiry that is necessary to ascertain whether the code has been violated;

(d) question an employee, without the employer being present, during the employee's regular hours of work, or otherwise to ascertain whether the code or an order under the code has been or is being complied with;

(e) require a person supplying information or giving oral or written statements to give any of them in the form of a written statement under oath;

(f) by notice in writing, demand the production of employment records for inspection either immediately or at a time, date, and place specified in the notice;

(g) on giving a receipt for it, remove any employment record for not more than 48 hours to make copies of it;

(h) by notice in writing, require an employer to record the times at which its employees start and stop work each day they work; and

(i) by notice in writing, require an employer to post notices, information bulletins, or extracts from the code at locations at the employer's place of business.

An officer may not enter a private dwelling without consent of the dwelling's occupier.

Every employer and employee is required to give whatever assistance is necessary for an officer to make an entry, inspection, investigation, or inquiry.

3. Order of director

The director may try to mediate the matter between the employer and the employee if an employee has been improperly dismissed or suspended —

(a) while on maternity leave or adoption leave,

(b) for making a complaint under the code or giving evidence in a matter under the code,

(c) because of a garnishee on his or her wages,

(d) because the employee demanded something to which the employee is entitled to under the code, or

(e) because the employee has made or must make a statement under the code.

If the director is unsuccessful in mediating the dispute, he or she may make an order requiring the employer to reinstate the employee and/or an order requiring payment not exceeding the amount the employee would have earned had the employee not been improperly dismissed or suspended.

4. Time of the complaint

An employee who is still employed by the employer about whom he or she has complained must obtain an order from the officer for wages and entitlements no later than one year after they were due but not paid by the employer. If the employee is no longer employed by the employer, an order must be obtained within one year from the date the employee's employment ended.

If an employee was improperly discharged or suspended for garnishee or complaint under the code, the director must make an order within one year from the date of the employee's discharge or suspension. In all instances, the director may extend the limitation period one year because of extenuating circumstances.

5. Appeal to umpire

Either the employee or the employer affected by the order served by an officer or a director may appeal the order to an umpire. Types of orders that may be appealed include:

(a) orders to pay wages or other entitlements,

(b) orders to reinstate an employee or pay money because of a wrongful dismissal or discharge,

(c) declarations that a business is being carried on by a common employer for the purposes of the code (see below),

(d) decisions that an employee is or is not exempted under the code because of managerial status, and

(e) permits authorizing payment below minimum wage for a handicapped person.

A common employer declaration is when, in the opinion of an officer, a business or other activity is carried on by two or more employers or other people. The officer may then make a declaration that all or any of the employers or people are a single employer for the purposes of the act.

For example, suppose an employee works for Company A, but is paid by Company B. The employee is then dismissed without cause from Company A. During an investigation, the officer might make a finding that Company A and Company B are common employers and hold both companies responsible for applicable severance pay.

The notice of appeal must be served on the director within 21 days of the date the decision being appealed was served. An umpire's order is final and binding.

6. Offences and penalties

It is an offence for any person to violate or fail to comply with an officer's notice or an order, award, permit, or certificate. If the order is not complied with, it may be filed in the Court of Queen's Bench and is then enforceable as an order of the court.

7. Director liability for unpaid wages

Despite any other legislation, the directors of a corporation are liable to an employee of the corporation for unpaid wages earned during a period not exceeding six months. A director is not liable if he or she was not a director when the unpaid wages were earned or if exempt from liability under the Alberta Business Corporations Act.

If an employment standards director finds that directors or former directors of a corporation are liable for payment of unpaid wages, the employment standards director may serve on each of the directors or previous directors of that corporation a certificate showing an order to pay unpaid wages. If the directors or previous directors do not file an appeal within 15 days, or if any appeal is unsuccessful, the director may file the certificate with the Court of Queen's Bench. The certificate is then enforceable as an order of the court.

A certificate may not be filed under this section against a director of a corporation more than two years after the date that person ceased to be a director.

3

WRONGFUL DISMISSAL

Employees who have been fired or who anticipate being fired are likely to undergo both financial and emotional stress. An understanding of some basic principles concerning wrongful dismissal will help with decision-making before and after any job termination. While the Employment Standards Code sets minimum standards for notice or pay in lieu of notice, an employee may be entitled to additional notice under the law. An employer saddled with an employee who demonstrates persistent incompetence, disloyalty, and insubordination may wish to review the law on what constitutes "just cause," and to determine what steps must be taken to fire an employee without breaking the law. However, wrongful dismissal is a complex, ever-changing area of law, and legal counsel is usually advisable for those people involved in a wrongful dismissal matter.

a. WHAT IS WRONGFUL DISMISSAL?

Wrongful dismissal is a legal concept that refers to the failure of an employer to provide an employee with either reasonable notice of termination of employment or pay in lieu of notice.

It is an implied term of every contract of employment, whether written or verbal, that an employer must give an employee either reasonable notice before termination of employment or salary in lieu of reasonable notice.

b. DISMISSAL FOR CAUSE

It is an implied term of every contract of employment, whether written or verbal, that the employer has a right to

44

dismiss the employee for cause. Cause implies that the employee has fundamentally breached his or her obligation to serve the employer faithfully.

Conduct amounting to cause gives the employer the right to dismiss an employee without giving reasonable notice of termination of employment or the money equivalent. Types of conduct that constitute cause include:

- Conflict of interest
- Dishonesty
- Disloyalty
- Insubordination
- Disobedience
- Neglect of duty
- Criminal or other immoral conduct
- Incompetence

Such acts by the employee destroy the basis of trust that must exist in an employment relationship.

An employee owes a duty of loyalty to the employer. Personal interests of the employee must not conflict with the employer. Directors, officers, and senior employees owe a higher duty of loyalty than other employees. Employees who owe a higher duty of loyalty are known as *fiduciaries*. Conduct that breaches the duty of loyalty include accepting kickbacks, setting up a personal business that competes with the employer's business, or obtaining loans from the employer for a family member without disclosing to the employer the family relationship or potential conflict of interest.

Sometimes cause is alleged to be the cumulative effect of past misconduct rather than one isolated incidence of misconduct. In that case, the employer must show that:

(a) the employee was warned that repetition of the conduct would lead to dismissal, and

(b) the employee was given reasonable time to improve her or his performance before being dismissed.

To be effective, the warning to the employee should be clear and in writing. While it may not be necessary to tell an employee he or she will be fired if the conduct does not improve, it is prudent for the employer to set out any consequences clearly.

If the conduct complained of is an isolated incidence of misconduct, it must be of such magnitude that it destroys the employment relationship.

c. CONDONATION

Condonation occurs whenever the employer, by the employer's behaviour, indicates to an employee that it is overlooking conduct that would constitute just cause for dismissal. If the employer condones or forgives certain conduct, either explicitly or through implication, it may be difficult to use that conduct in the future as the basis for dismissing for cause.

The most common instance of condonation is where the employee commits a wrongful act or omission and the employer does nothing. If the employer continues to employ the employee for any considerable time after discovering the misconduct, the employer is considered to be condoning the employee's conduct. The employer cannot afterward dismiss for that fault alone. The longer the period of condonation, the greater the obligation of the employer to give very specific and definite warnings before dismissing the employee.

d. CONSTRUCTIVE DISMISSAL

Constructive dismissal occurs when the employer, without the employee's consent:

(a) fundamentally changes the employee's existing job to the employee's detriment, or

(b) the employer moves the employee to a new job, fundamentally changing the nature of the employment to the employee's detriment.

If an employer fundamentally changes an employee's job to that employee's detriment and the employee subsequently resigns, the employer's conduct may still constitute wrongful dismissal. If changes in the duties and responsibilities of the employee's existing job go to the very root of the job, such a change will likely constitute a wrongful dismissal. If the employer's motivation for changing the employee's job is economic survival, the change may not constitute wrongful dismissal unless there is humiliation or decrease in authority for the employee.

1. Reduction in salary or benefits

A reduction in salary imposed on the employee and without proper cause has been held by the courts to be constructive dismissal. However, the courts may not view a minor change only in pay as a fundamental change. A change in benefits may also constitute wrongful dismissal. In one case, taking away an employee's company car was considered to amount to wrongful dismissal.

2. Demotion

A change amounting to a demotion may amount to constructive dismissal. A demotion is generally characterized by a downward change in pay or status. For example, if an employee is asked to return to a job he or she had previously held or is asked to accept a position of lower rank, such a job change would likely constitute a form of constructive dismissal.

3. Geographical transfer

Whether a geographical transfer of an employee amounts to constructive dismissal depends on the circumstances of each case. If the employment contract between the parties contemplates relocation, the employee must accept a relocation according to the terms of the contract. The court will look at factors including:

    (a) whether job transfers are a way of life in the particular company,

    (b) job level of employee and any agreement by that employee to previous transfers,

    (c) existence of hardship to the employee to relocate,

    (d) employer's size and number of branches, and

    (e) good faith of the employer.

e. WHAT IS REASONABLE NOTICE?

Whenever an employer hires an employee for an indefinite period, there is an implied term in the employment contract that the employee is entitled to reasonable notice of termination of employment. The notice period is to allow the employee opportunity to find comparable employment. However, few employers choose to continue to employ a worker during a lengthy notice period since productivity and morale are bound to suffer. Most employers dismiss without notice but pay damages in lieu of notice.

Standard factors used in calculating length of reasonable notice include:

    (a) age, where older employees are entitled to longer notice;

    (b) type of employment, where more senior level employees are entitled to longer notice;

    (c) length of service, where longer service employees are entitled to longer notice;

    (d) availability of similar employment, where lack of available, similar employment entitles the employee to longer notice; and

(e) enticement, where if the employee was enticed by the employer from previous secure employment and dismissed shortly thereafter, the court is more likely to treat the employee as a long-service employee in terms of notice required.

Often, the courts will not award unskilled or semi-skilled wage earners notice significantly greater than that which the Employment Standards Code provides. However, a senior manager, vice president, or president could be entitled to notice of up to two years. Certain rules of thumb apply:

(a) junior unskilled or semi-skilled employees with five years of service or less are entitled to notice equal to one week's salary for every year of service;

(b) semi-skilled employees or skilled employees with more than five years of service are entitled to two weeks' notice for every year of service;

(c) management employees with up to 15 years of service are entitled to one month's notice for every year of service; and

(d) highly paid senior executives are entitled to six to eight weeks' notice for every year of service, with a minimum of one year's notice.

f. MITIGATION

A wrongfully dismissed employee has a duty to take all reasonable steps to mitigate — or lessen — his or her damages. The employee must make an honest and reasonable effort to find comparable employment. However, only those steps that a reasonable and prudent person would take in the circumstances are required. While the employee has the initial burden of proving that he or she has made reasonable efforts to mitigate damages, the final onus rests on the employer to prove the employee did not sufficiently mitigate.

The employer must show a lack of effort on the employee's part and the availability of similar employment.

Since the courts attempt to place the employee in the same financial position as he or she would have been before the wrongful dismissal, any subsequent damage award the court has ordered will be reduced by any income the employee earned during the reasonable notice period the court has set. If the employee fails to search honestly and reasonably for comparable employment, the damages awarded will be reduced accordingly.

Whether an employee has fulfilled the duty to mitigate depends on the facts of each case. Each case must be judged on its merits.

Expert testimony on the probability of finding employment and copies of job advertisements may help prove that jobs were available to the employee. Similarly, the employer may wish to submit evidence that the employee unreasonably refused a job offer.

g. DAMAGES

An employee hired for an indefinite time who is dismissed without just cause is entitled to receive reasonable notice of dismissal. If the employer does not give reasonable notice or pay in lieu of reasonable notice, a court will award damages to the employee to compensate for the breach of contract.

The general principle of damages in breach of contract cases is to put the employee in the same position he or she would have been if the contract had not been breached. In evaluating damages, the courts consider all salary and benefits, including company cars, club fees, bonuses, profit sharing, pension rights, and vacation pay that the employee would have received had he or she continued working through the notice period.

1. Salary

An employee is entitled to the salary he or she would have earned during the period of reasonable notice. Some cases have successfully argued that the employee is entitled to the benefit of any salary increments that the employer would have routinely granted during the reasonable notice period.

2. Bonuses

Does the employee have a contractual right to a bonus during the notice period if a bonus incentive plan or profit sharing plan is in place? If no contractual right exists, and if it is at the employer's discretion whether to pay the bonus or not, no bonus is due as part of the damages for wrongful dismissal.

3. Pension and other benefits

The reduction of pension benefits are taken into account when assessing damages; however the courts are divided over the method to use to calculate the loss. One issue is whether the employee should be compensated for either the loss based on contributions the employer would have made during the reasonable notice period or for the loss of pension benefits the employee would have received on retirement. Given the complexity of this problem, it is important to receive expert advice if you are in this situation.

Damages for loss of insurance and medical plans are also properly included in an award for wrongful dismissal. Again, expert advice should be sought for the calculation of these damages.

An employee may or may not be successful in claiming costs incurred in searching for alternative employment. The courts are also divided over the issue of whether an employee may include as damages the expense of moving to another city to obtain comparable employment.

Other losses that the courts may decide the employee will be compensated for include club membership fees, company car or car allowance, and vacation pay that would have been earned during the notice period.

4. Mental distress and other aggravated damages

Damages for mental distress, including pain, grief, and damaged self-esteem, are awarded based on the employer's harsh manner of dismissing the employee. The employee may be entitled to a claim for damages for mental distress if the court decides that:

(a) the period of notice was not reasonable,

(b) the employer did not have just cause to dismiss the employee, and

(c) the employer's actions caused the employee mental distress.

Generally, aggravated damages will not likely be awarded unless the employer's conduct amounts to a separate actionable wrong. Where this occurs the employer's action can be brought to court for a reason other than wrongful dismissal. A separate actionable wrong includes defamation of the employee after dismissal and continued unfounded allegations of just cause.

5. Punitive damages

Punitive damages are rarely awarded for wrongful dismissals. The Supreme Court of Canada has held that punitive damages may be awarded only for conduct that is deserving of punishment because of its harsh, vindictive, and malicious nature.

As with aggravated damages, there must be a separate actionable wrong before punitive damages will be awarded. In one case, an employer dismissed an employee without cause under a cloud of an unfounded criminal investigation. The employer was found liable for punitive damages and was required to pay additional money to the employee over and above compensatory damages. Similarly, when an employer defamed an employee subsequent to dismissing that employee, punitive damages were awarded in favour of the employee.

4

HUMAN RIGHTS PROTECTION

The extent to which human rights are protected in the workplace represents an important measure of our community standards. What questions is an employer permitted to ask in a job interview? What questions can a prospective employee refuse to answer on the grounds that the questions violate the Human Rights, Multiculturalism and Citizenship Act?

An employer has a duty to accommodate his or her employee's physical, religious, and other need, as they apply to the workplace. However, some employee demands may pose undue hardship on the employer, and the employer does not have to accommodate such demands.

Regulating against sexual harassment has gained important new ground in the last decade. Exposure of the issue in the media, advocacy by women's groups, and the impact of decisions by courts and human rights commissions across the country have caused more women to speak out when sexually harassed.

Men are also victims of sexual harassment, though the majority of cases involve women. Sexual harassment signifies abuse of power. Men still hold more powerful positions in the work force than women, thus spawning more opportunities for the abuse of power by men than women.

a. THE ALBERTA HUMAN RIGHTS, CITIZENSHIP AND MULTICULTURALISM ACT

1. Recent amendments to Alberta human rights legislation

The Alberta human rights legislation, formerly called the Individual's Rights Protection Act, has been renamed the Alberta Human Rights, Citizenship and Multiculturalism Act. There were three major amendments incorporated into the new act:

(a) The act identifies family status, marital status, and source of income as three new grounds of protection.

(b) The time limit for making a complaint of discrimination to the Alberta Human Rights and Citizenship Commission has been extended from 6 months to 12 months from the date of the alleged incident.

(c) Complaints are now heard by a human rights panel.

2. Grounds of discrimination

The act prohibits discrimination on certain grounds. The part of the act dealing with discrimination in employment has an impact on both employees and employers. The act states that no employer may dismiss, discriminate against in the workplace, or refuse to hire any person on the grounds of:

(a) race,

(b) religious beliefs (including native spirituality),

(c) colour,

(d) gender (which includes sexual harassment and pregnancy),

(e) physical disability,

(f) mental disability,

(g) age,

(h) ancestry,

(i) place of origin,

(j) family status,

(k) marital status, or

(l) source of income.

Unlike some other provincial and federal human rights legislation, sexual orientation is not a ground for protection under Alberta's new act.

3. Three new grounds of protection

As noted above, employees now enjoy the added protection that employers cannot dismiss, discriminate against in the workplace, or refuse to hire on the basis of family status, marital status, or source of income.

(a) *Family status.* The act defines family status as the status of being related to another person by blood, marriage, or adoption.

(b) *Marital status.* Marital status refers to the status of being married, single, widowed, divorced, separated, or living with a person of the opposite sex in a conjugal relationship outside marriage. Thus, an employer may not discriminate against a person because he or she is living in a common-law relationship.

(c) *Source of income.* Source of income refers to lawful source of income, including pensions and social assistance benefits (welfare).

4. Duty to accommodate and undue hardship

An employer's duty to accommodate the employee arises in cases of direct and adverse effect or indirect discrimination. Adverse effect or indirect discrimination occurs when a workplace rule, though neutral on its face, has an unfavourable impact on one of the groups protected by the legislation. For example, consider a hearing-impaired person who cannot complete a work task because a ringing bell communicates instructions. The employer may have a duty to accommodate the employee by replacing the ringing bell with a flashing light. While the ringing bell instruction is not direct discrimination by the employer, it *is* indirect discrimination, and the employer has a duty to accommodate the employee up to the point of undue hardship on the employer.

The Supreme Court has stated that undue hardship signifies more than minor inconvenience to the employer. Exactly what constitutes undue hardship for the employer is assessed on a case-by-case basis. Factors taken into account include financial cost, potential disruption of an existing collective agreement, size of the workplace, employee morale, and flexibility of the work force. For example, if an employee cannot work on a certain day because of his or her religious beliefs, the issue of undue hardship would be assessed by determining how difficult it is for that particular employer to transfer the shift to another employee.

5. Employer defences

(a) Bona fide occupational requirement

The act states that discrimination on the basis of any of the protected grounds is not prohibited if the refusal, limitation, specification, or preference is based on a bona fide occupational requirement (BFOR).

The test for what constitutes a BFOR has both a subjective and an objective element. From a subjective standpoint, the employer must honestly believe that the requirement is necessary for reasons of safety and economy. From an objective standpoint, the requirement must be reasonably necessary to ensure performance of the job without risking the safety of others.

For example, a moving company's requirement that employees retire at 60 constitutes direct discrimination on the basis of age, a protected ground under the act. However, if the employer can show both subjectively and objectively that there are bona fide reasons for the limitation, the employer is not in violation of the act. The burden of proving a BFOR rests with the employer.

(b) Reasonable and justifiable contravention

The act states that discrimination will not be considered unlawful if the employer can demonstrate that the discrimination was reasonable and justifiable in the circumstances.

For example, in 1992, the Supreme Court of Canada held that the policy of the University of Alberta to require mandatory retirement at age 65 discriminated against faculty employees on the basis of age. However, the policy was held to be reasonable and justifiable in the circumstances.

In another case, the Alberta Human Rights and Citizenship Commission held that an employer's firing of an employee with AIDS for fear of contracting AIDS in the workplace constituted discrimination on the basis of physical disability. The employer's belief was held to be unreasonable and unjustifiable in light of existing medical knowledge.

6. Protection from pre-employment inquiries

The act provides protection for employees from certain pre-employment inquiries. No person may use or circulate any form of application for employment, publish any advertisement for employment, or make any written or oral inquiry of an applicant that discriminates on the basis of any of the protected grounds described in the act.

As well, an employer is not entitled to ask for any information about the protected grounds. Exceptions will be made if the employer can prove the existence of a BFOR. The commission has published guidelines for pre-employment situations, which are summarized below.

(a) The employer may not request photographs. Photographs can be used to discriminate on the basis of protected grounds such as race, colour, gender, physical disabilities, or ancestry. A photograph can be requested only after an offer of employment has been made and accepted.

(b) No questions may be asked about religious beliefs.

(c) The applicant may not be asked questions requiring disclosure of gender as part of the answer.

(d) The employer cannot make inquiries about the state of the applicant's health or disabilities. Employers should give enough information on the job description to allow prospective employees to assess their own suitability.

A job-related medical exam may be conducted before an employment offer is made. It is permissible to ask for a declaration from the applicant, such as, "I understand that a job-related medical examination may be required and that the offer of employment may be contingent on a satisfactory job-related medical examination."

(e) Psychological evaluations are permitted only if there is a demonstrated need for the information. For example, an applicant to the police force may be required to take such tests because of the stressful nature of police work.

(f) The employer may not ask the age of an applicant but may ask if the applicant is of the age of majority (18 years or older).

(g) The employer may ask for previous addresses in Canada only.

(h) Questions about citizenship are prohibited. However, the employer may ask, "Are you legally entitled to work in Canada?" or "Are you either a Canadian citizen or a landed immigrant?"

(i) The employer may not question an applicant on marital status, number of children, child care arrangements, or future family plans. It is okay to ask whether the employee can accommodate the work schedule.

(j) The employer may not ask questions about an applicant's marital status. This precludes questions about child care arrangements and a person's maiden name.

If the employer wants a previous name for reference checks, a request for the name should be phrased, "Names used in previous employment for the purposes of reference check." If the employer wants names for notification in case of emergency, questions should be phrased, "Person to notify in case of an emergency?" Ideally, this information should be requested after employment has been offered and accepted.

(k) Fluency in languages may be asked about only if relevant to the job.

(l) Care needs to be used when asking information about schools attended and clubs or organization memberships. It may be prudent for an employer to include a statement on the application form stating that the applicant need not disclose any information that could indicate race, religion, colour, place of origin, or physical and mental disabilities.

(m) Employers may not ask about a prospective employee's workers' compensation history.

(n) Questions about foreign military service are prohibited, as they could result in disclosure of information on prohibited grounds. (For example, if a person is asked where he or she served in the military outside the country, the person's answer would likely reveal the country of origin or ancestry.)

7. Sexual harassment

The commission defines sexual harassment in the workplace as:

> Any unwelcome behaviour, sexual in nature, that adversely affects, or threatens to affect, directly or indirectly, a person's job security, working conditions or prospects for promotion or earnings, or prevents a person from getting a job.

Sexual harassment is discrimination on the ground of gender. It is not listed as a separate ground for discrimination in the act since it is included under the ground of gender. Sexual harassment is one of the most frequent complaints human rights agencies receive.

(a) What constitutes sexual harassment?

Conduct that constitutes sexual harassment includes:

- Unwelcome physical conduct, such as pinching, hugging, brushing up against, or patting

- Unwelcome sexual requests, remarks, jokes, leering, and whistling

- Unfair evaluations or reprimands, reduced working hours, discipline or dismissal as a form of retaliation for refusal to submit to sexual harassment

There is a profound difference between sexual harassment and innocent flirtation or office romance. Mutual attraction does not cause discomfort to any of the parties involved. Sexual harassment, on the other hand, is behaviour that is unwanted and coercive by one of the parties. It is usually one person's attempt to exercise power over another. Sexual harassment is unwelcome behaviour that the harasser knew or ought to have known would be objectionable.

(b) Employer responsibility

The Supreme Court ruled in a 1985 landmark case that employers are automatically liable in their own name for acts of sexual harassment of its employees, managers, or representatives, whether or not the employer knew or ought reasonably to have known that the sexual harassment was taking place. The employer is said to be *vicariously liable* for the sexual harassment its employees commit. Even if fault cannot be proven against the employer, the employer is still responsible. Given this potential for liability, employers have incentive to take active steps to eliminate sexual harassment. Such steps might include adopting special education programs, introducing effective complaints procedures, and dismissing or disciplining those employees who commit sexual harassment.

An employer cannot escape liability on the basis of *due diligence*. That is, the employer is still liable even if it has acted reasonably and with the diligence required in the circumstances. However, if the employer has taken steps to eliminate sexual harassment, such steps will likely reduce the penalty the human rights panel imposes. The commission states in its published policies that an employer's liability for sexual harassment may be increased if no effective sexual harassment policy exists in the workplace. Prompt, appropriate action if there are complaints may reduce employer liability further. The commission also has useful suggestions for employers wishing to develop an effective sexual harassment policy, including a sample sexual harassment policy.

(c) Complaint process for sexual harassment

The first thing a person should do if he or she is being sexually harassed is tell the harasser to stop. This is especially important because the onus lies on the complainant to prove that the behaviour was unwelcome and objectionable. If that doesn't stop the abuse, the employee should ask the employer to implement the employer's sexual harassment policy. If the employer fails to respond appropriately, the complainant should contact the commission. It may sometimes be appropriate to contact a union representative or, if there was any assault, the police.

The time limit for making a complaint of discrimination to the commission has been extended from six months to one year from the date of the incident. It is important to document the incidents relating to the harassment, with details on where and how it happened, including names of witnesses if available.

8. Harassment on grounds other than gender

Sexual harassment is a well-known offence. However, harassment can also occur when one person subjects another to unwelcome verbal or physical conduct on the basis of his or her race, religious beliefs, colour, gender, physical or mental disability, age, ancestry, or place of origin. Examples of harassment include jokes, derogatory remarks, or taunts about appearance or beliefs. As with sexual harassment, an employer may be vicariously liable for harassment offences its employees commit.

9. Equal pay for equal work

If employees of both sexes perform the same or substantially similar work for an employer, that employer must pay the employees at the same rate of pay. Furthermore, an employer may not reduce the rate of pay of an employee in order to comply with the act. The act gives the employee the right to claim the difference in wages between the amount paid and the amount that should have been paid to the employee.

Any pay differentials between men and women must be based on factors other than gender. Those factors may include experience, education, and merit. In previous cases, the commission has held that work done by men and women need not be precisely the same before equal pay provisions apply, but need only be substantially similar. For example, the commission held that an employer violated the act by paying a woman less as a second-year apprentice wood-worker than that amount paid to a male first-year apprentice.

10. Pregnancy

The act specifically provides that protection against discrimination on the basis of gender includes pregnancy. An employer may not fire, lay off, or demote a woman for being pregnant. As well, an employer may not ask a prospective employee if she is pregnant or planning to have children.

Under the Alberta Employment Standards Code, a woman is entitled to 18 weeks of maternity leave so long as the employee meets requirements of employer notice and medical certificates. (See chapter 2 for a more detailed discussion of maternity leave and parental benefits.)

Pregnancy-based discrimination is a frequent ground of complaint. Employers must treat women who are pregnant and unable to work for health-related reasons the same way they do other disabled or sick employees. If disability benefits are paid to sick employees, those benefits must be paid also to pregnant women who are sick; it does not matter whether the sickness is pregnancy-related. This holds even if the employee is sick while pregnant and entitled to maternity leave.

While portions of a maternity leave are considered voluntary, the period during which the employee is in labour, giving birth, and immediately following birth will likely be considered a health-related absence. The employee must provide medical evidence that she was unable to work for the time she is claiming benefits. The Alberta Employment Standards Code bars employment for six weeks after the birth of a child unless there is medical evidence of fitness to resume work. This provision bolsters the argument that at least part of a maternity leave is a health-related absence.

Where possible, an employer must try to accommodate a pregnant employee in the workplace. For example, an employer should try to excuse a pregnant employee from lifting heavy boxes. However, it would then be reasonable for that employer to ask the pregnant employee to absorb extra non-physical duties in exchange.

11. Physical and mental disability

The act states:

> "Physical disability" means any degree of physical disability, infirmity, malformation or disfigurement that is caused by bodily injury, birth defect or illness and, without limiting the generality of the foregoing, includes epilepsy, paralysis, amputation, lack of physical coordination, blindness or visual impediment, deafness or hearing impediment, muteness or speech impediment, and physical reliance on a guide dog, wheelchair or other remedial appliance or device.
>
> "Mental disability" means any mental disorder, developmental disorder or learning disorder, regardless of the cause or duration of the disorder.

Employers are expected to accommodate employees who are disabled unless it would cause the employer undue hardship. For example, if retaining a disabled employee would create a health or safety risk, such an accommodation would be considered undue hardship for the employer. The onus of proving undue hardship is on the employer.

The commission recognizes alcoholism and drug addiction as disabilities. While an employer has a duty to accommodate an alcoholic employee, the employee has a corresponding duty to genuinely try to benefit from the treatment he or she is receiving. Employers should have policies on workplace issues, including alcoholism and drug testing.

12. Drug and alcohol testing

Blanket drug testing of employees or prospective employees is not condoned by the commission. Prospective employees may be tested only if there is a job-related reason. Tests should be given to employees only if there is a reasonable suspicion of an impaired ability to perform job duties safely and satisfactorily.

13. Dress code

According to the act, employers can set appearance and grooming standards that are reasonable, not arbitrary, and not used to discriminate against any particular group. If conditions of employment interfere with employee religious practices or employee physical well-being, the employer should consider changing those work conditions to accommodate the employee.

14. Complaint process, investigations, and remedies

Legal counsel is optional for a complainant lodging a complaint with the commission. A complaint must be made within 12 months of the alleged incident. For violations that occurred before July 15, 1996, the complaint must be made within six months.

On receiving a complaint, the commission forwards a copy of it to the employer. Some cases are settled voluntarily by the parties at this early stage. Otherwise, a conciliator appointed by the commission will try to bring about a resolution. If there is no settlement within 30 days, an investigator is assigned. Investigators have broad powers, including the right to enter any place at any reasonable time, the right to make inquiries of people with information relevant to the subject matter of the investigation, and the right to demand to see documents.

After investigation, a report to either dismiss or uphold the complaint is prepared for the director of the commission to review. The director will dismiss any complaint that is without merit.

The director may discontinue a valid complaint if the complainant refuses to accept a reasonable settlement. A complainant may appeal a dismissal or discontinuance to the chief commissioner within 30 days. The chief commissioner's decision is final and binding, subject to the judicial review by the Court of Queen's Bench.

The director may refer complaints with merit to the human rights panel if the employee and employer cannot settle the matter. The human rights panel consists of one or more commissioners. The decision of the panel has the same effect as a decision of the Court of Queen's Bench. The decision can be appealed to the Court of Queen's Bench within 30 days.

The act specifically provides protection from retaliation against a person who has filed a complaint or assisted anyone in filing a complaint.

If the complaint is partly or wholly justified, the panel may order the employer to do any or all of the following:

(a) stop the conduct constituting a violation under the act,

(b) refrain from future violation, and

(c) compensate the complainant for any wages or expenses lost as a result of the violation.

The panel may also make any other order necessary to place the complainant in the same position he or she would have been but for the violation. Remedies include a cease and desist order, an award of lost wages, an apology, the implementation of an anti-discrimination policy, and employer attendance at an educational workshop.

b. THE CANADIAN HUMAN RIGHTS ACT

1. Who is protected?

The Canadian Human Rights Act protects the equality rights of Canadians on a federal level. It applies to the following organizations:

- Federal departments, agencies, and crown corporations
- Canada Post
- Chartered banks
- National airlines
- Interprovincial communications and telephone companies
- Interprovincial transportation companies
- Other federally regulated industries, such as certain mining operations

2. What grounds are protected in the workplace?

As with the Alberta legislation, the Canadian Human Rights Act prohibits employment discrimination in both pre-employment situations and during employment. The grounds include:

(a) race,

(b) religious beliefs,

(c) colour,

(d) sex (including pregnancy and childbirth),

(e) physical disability (including dependence on drugs and alcohol),

(f) mental disability,

(g) age,

(h) national or ethnic origin,

(i) family status,

(j) marital status, and

(k) criminal conviction for which a pardon has been granted.

The Ontario Court of Appeal also considers sexual orientation a protected ground even though it is not explicitly set out in the act.

Discrimination is not considered a discriminatory practice under the act if it is based on a bona fide occupational requirement (BFOR) (see section a.5. above for a discussion of BFORs).

3. The Canadian Human Rights Commission

The Canadian Human Rights Commission administers the Canadian Human Rights Act. The commission decides on individual complaints and approves commission policies. The commission also investigates complaints of discrimination and complaints alleging unequal pay for work of equal value. As well, the commission monitors reports that federally regulated employers submit under the Employment Equity Act and takes action based on those reports when necessary.

4. Complaint process

If a complaint cannot be settled in the early stages, a report is prepared for commission review. The commission may dismiss the complaint, appoint a conciliator, or send the complaint to a human rights tribunal. If a conciliator is appointed, he or she tries to settle the complaint by reaching an agreement between the employer and employee. If no agreement is reached, the case is returned to the commission for review. The commission then may dismiss the case or send it the human rights tribunal for adjudication. Remedies for complaints include reinstatement, compensation for lost wages, letters of apology, and the requirement of employers to implement anti-harassment policies.

Tribunal decisions may be appealed to a review tribunal set up under the act or to the Federal Court, depending on the circumstances. Review tribunal decisions may be appealed to the Federal Court.

c. THE EMPLOYMENT EQUITY ACT

Employment equity helps ensure that designated groups long under-represented in the workplace get a fair chance at jobs and promotions. Those designated groups are —

(a) women,

(b) aboriginal people,

(c) people with disabilities, and

(d) visible minorities.

The act requires federally regulated companies with 100 or more employees to take action against discrimination.

These companies must identify and eliminate barriers to the employment of designated group members, institute special measures to ensure these people are proportionately represented in the work force, and report results annually to Human Resources Development Canada.

In their reports, employers must provide details on the number of women, people with disabilities, members of visible minorities, and aboriginal people at various organizational levels. These reports are then forwarded to the Canadian Human Rights Commission. The commission may launch investigations and file complaints on the basis of the information provided.

Employers are expected to examine all employment policies and practices to identify and remove barriers to the recruitment, hiring, retention, treatment, and promotion of members of these four designated groups. Each employer must also produce an employment equity plan for correcting under-representation in the work force. The object is for employers to remove past discriminatory practices and actively remedy imbalances in their work force.

The act does not apply to provincially regulated companies.

d. THE CHARTER OF RIGHTS AND FREEDOMS

All human rights, employment standards, labour relations, and other employment statutes can be constitutionally challenged on the grounds of violation of one or more of the rights and freedoms guaranteed by the Canadian Charter of Rights and Freedoms. The Charter forms part of the Constitution Act, 1982.

Neither the provinces nor the federal government has the power to interfere with the basic rights set out in the Charter except through constitutional amendment. These basic rights are said to be entrenched in the constitution. A person who feels that his or her rights have been interfered with by legislation or other forms of government action can rely on the basic rights and freedoms protected by the Charter to seek redress in the courts.

1. When does the Charter apply?

The Charter applies only to public matters. It applies to all government agencies and organizations, including municipalities, that are exercising statutory authority. An individual can apply to court for a declaration that his or her Charter rights have been violated by legislation, regulations, laws, or the acts of public servants.

Private matters between individuals, corporations, or even government-funded organizations acting in a private capacity, such as schools and hospitals, are covered by provincial human rights legislation.

There are two important limitations on the entrenchment of basic rights. Section 1 of the Charter states that the

71

listed rights and freedoms can be interfered with if doing so could be "demonstrably justified in a free and democratic society." Individual judges must decide what is justifiable and what is not.

The second limitation, in section 33 of the Charter, states that certain rights can be overridden by the legislature. While our courts do have control over the protection of some Charter rights, politicians in the legislature have final say in the control of others.

2. Charter rights and employment

Everyone is granted fundamental freedoms, including the freedom of conscience and religion. This is granted in section 2 of the Charter. Section 6 grants every citizen of Canada and every person who has the status of a permanent resident of Canada the right to pursue the gaining of a livelihood in any provinces. Sections 15 and 28 state:

> (15)1 Every individual is equal before and under the law and has the right to the equal protection and equal benefit of the law without discrimination and, in particular, without discrimination based on race, national or ethnic origin, colour, religion, sex, age or mental or physical disability.

> (28) Notwithstanding anything in this Charter, the rights and freedoms referred to in it are guaranteed equally to male and female persons.

3. Sexual orientation and the Charter

In the Alberta case *Vriend v. Alberta*, Mr. Vriend took the Alberta legislature to court on the grounds that the government offended section 15 of the Charter by failing to include sexual orientation as a prohibited ground of discrimination in the Alberta Individual's Rights Protection Act (now named the Alberta Human Rights, Citizenship and Multiculturalism Act). Mr. Vriend was fired upon the employer's discovery that he was homosexual. The trial judge found in favour of Mr. Vriend.

On appeal, the Court of Appeal found that the omission of the ground of sexual orientation does not amount to government action that can be challenged under the Charter. The court held that the act, in its silence, relegates an issue of private conduct to private, rather than government, resolution. The Court of Appeal was unwilling to interfere with the Alberta legislature's decision not to provide homosexuals protection against discrimination. Mr. Vriend obtained leave to appeal his case to the Supreme Court of Canada. As of June 1997, the Supreme Court had heard the case and had reserved judgment.

5

HEALTH AND SAFETY PROTECTION — THE OCCUPATIONAL HEALTH AND SAFETY ACT

Health and safety of our workers is critical to a productive and efficient work force. Most employers and employees are aware that serious accidents must be reported to the director of inspection as soon as they can be. Perhaps less widely known is the requirement to keep a report of potential accidents for two years on the work premises.

If an employee believes on reasonable grounds that the assigned work poses an imminent danger to himself or herself, or to others, the employee is entitled to stop working and must report this situation to the employer as soon as possible. If the employer does not respond appropriately, the employee may file a complaint under the Occupational Health and Safety Act. The Occupational Health and Safety Act establishes standards for the protection and promotion of employees' health and safety throughout the province.

a. REGULATIONS UNDER THE ACT

Regulations under the Occupational Health and Safety Act are comprehensive, and both employees and employers have an obligation to be familiar with all regulations relevant to their particular work site. These regulations include:

- Chemical Hazards Regulation
- Designated Work Sites Order Regulation
- Explosives Safety Regulation

- Farming and Ranching Exemption Regulation
- First Aid Regulation
- General Safety Regulation
- Joint Work Site Health and Safety Committee Regulation
- Mines Safety Regulation
- Noise Regulation
- Ventilation Regulation

b. TO WHOM DOES THE ACT APPLY?

The act affects most employees and employers in Alberta. Employers subject to the act include self-employed people, people who employ one or more employees, and directors and officers of a corporation who oversee the occupational health and safety of employees the corporation employs. The major exceptions include farmers (including fruit, vegetable, and crop farmers, and keepers of bees), certain agricultural workers, domestic workers, federal government employees, and employees in industry regulated by the federal government. Occupational health and safety for federally regulated employers is subject to the Canada Labour Code.

1. Obligation of the employer

Every employer must, as far as it reasonably can, ensure the health and safety of its employees. As well, the employer must ensure that the employees are aware of their responsibilities and duties under the act and regulations.

2. Obligation of the employee

The employee has a reciprocal obligation to take reasonable care to protect the health and safety of himself or herself and to cooperate with the employer to protect health and safety in the workplace.

3. Obligation of the supplier

The supplier must ensure, as far as it reasonably can, that any tool, appliance, or equipment that it supplies is in safe operating condition. As well, suppliers must ensure that any tool, appliance, equipment, or hazardous material that it supplies complies with the act and regulations.

4. Obligation of the contractor

Contractors that direct operations of an employer must ensure, as far as it reasonably can, that the employer complies with the act and regulations.

c. SERIOUS INJURIES AND ACCIDENTS

Certain accidents and injuries must be reported to the director of inspection as soon as possible. These injuries and accidents include:

(a) any injury or accident that results in death,

(b) serious injury or accident resulting in a two-day or longer hospital stay, and

(c) collapse of certain equipment or certain structural failures.

If an accident occurs that has the potential to cause injury, the employer must:

(a) investigate the accident,

(b) prepare a report including a description of preventative measures taken,

(c) have a copy of the report available for a health and safety officer to inspect, and

(d) keep the report for two years.

If there is an accident, a health and safety officer may investigate the scene of the accident. Officers have broad powers to remedy unsafe or unhealthy conditions, including orders for work stoppage and equipment seizure. The officer may solicit information from anyone present at the time of the accident and may seize any substances or equipment relating to the accident. If appropriate, the officer will try to achieve voluntary compliance with the employer after an accident. If the employer does not comply voluntarily, an order will be issued.

A director of Medical Services may require an employee to be medically examined by a Medical Services doctor or the employee's doctor to determine the extent of injury. The examination will be at the employer's expense.

If an employee is employed in a hazardous occupation or at a hazardous work site, a director of Medical Services may require the employer to register the employee's name and the location of the work site with the director. In addition, the employee may be required to have regular medical examinations to monitor the employee's health. A director of Medical Services may also order the regular inspection of certain work sites.

d. IMMINENT DANGER AND WORK STOPPAGE

Under the act, an employee may not continue to work if there is imminent danger to himself or herself or to other employees. Imminent danger means any danger that is not normal for that occupation or a danger under which the person would not normally carry out his or her work. An example of imminent danger is a situation in which an employee is asked to enter or work in a trench that is more than five feet deep and is not protected by either shoring or cutbacks.

If the employee stops working or using equipment because of imminent danger, the employee must notify the employer as soon as possible. Once notified, the employer must investigate and eliminate the danger.

An employer may not stop paying the employee or take any disciplinary action against an employee who stops work because of imminent danger. If an employer fails to respond appropriately, the employee may file a complaint under the act.

e. PROHIBITION AGAINST DISCIPLINARY ACTION

An employer may not dismiss or take any other disciplinary action against an employee for acting in compliance with the act, regulation, or orders. If an employee feels he or she has been wrongly disciplined or dismissed, that employee may file a complaint with an officer.

The officer will prepare a written record of the employee's complaint. A copy of the record is provided to both the employer and employee. Either the employer or the employee may request the Occupational Health and Safety Council to review the matter by serving a notice of appeal on a director of inspection within 30 days after receiving the record. After hearing the matter, council may:

(a) reinstate the employee to his or her former employment,

(b) have disciplinary action stopped,

(c) order the employer to pay the employee wages the employee would have earned but for dismissal or disciplinary action, and/or

(d) remove a reprimand on the employee's work record.

If the employee or employer wants to appeal the council's decision, an appeal must be made to the Court of Queen's Bench.

f. REPORTS FOR HAZARDOUS SUBSTANCES

Both the Occupational Health and Safety Act and the Chemical Hazards Regulation require that employers maintain an inventory of all hazardous materials that may be present in the workplace. It must be updated once a year. If any hazardous substance is used, stored, or manufactured at or on a work site, the employer must provide a written report; specific forms employers must fill out are available from the office of the Director of Occupational Hygiene. As well, the contractor or employer responsible for the work site must ensure:

(a) the product is labelled in accordance with the regulations,

(b) a material safety data sheet for the product is available to the employees on the site, and

(c) an employee who works with a hazardous product or close to a hazardous product receives education, instruction, or training about the product.

An employer must also ensure that each employee's exposure by inhalation to any hazardous substances listed in the regulations is kept as low as is reasonably practicable and does not exceed its occupational exposure limits for chemical substances.

If employees are exposed to certain hazardous products, the health of those employees must be monitored. If a worker is employed in a hazardous occupation or at a hazardous work site, a director of Medical Services may —

(a) require that the worker's employer, within 30 days of the beginning of the worker's employment, register with a director the worker's name and the location of the work site where he or she is employed;

(b) require the worker to have regular medical examinations (paid for by the employer);

(c) prescribe the type and frequency of the medical examinations;

(d) prescribe the form and content of medical records to be complied for that worker, and

(e) prescribe the period for which those medical records must be maintained.

When a person registered with a director terminates his or her employment with the employer, the employer must notify a director of Medical Services of that termination within 30 days.

g. JOINT WORK SITE HEALTH AND SAFETY COMMITTEES

The Minister of Labour may order that a joint work site health and safety committee be established. The committee identifies unhealthy or unsafe conditions on the work site, makes recommendations for improvement, and establishes training programs.

h. APPEAL

Appeal of any officer's order may be made to the Occupational Health and Safety Council by serving a notice of appeal on a director of inspection within 30 days of the date the order being appealed was served on the person appealing. The council hears the appeal and renders a decision as soon as possible.

The Court of Queen's Bench hears appeals of a council's order on questions of law or questions of jurisdiction (i.e., whether the council has authority to make the particular decision). The Court of Queen's Bench may make any order it considers appropriate.

i. OFFENCES

Any person who violates the act or regulations, or fails to comply with an order, is guilty of an offence. For a first offence, the fine may be up to $150 000 with a jail term of up to six months. If it is a continuing offence, a person may receive a further fine of up to $10 000 for each day.

For a second offence, the fine is up to $300 000 and imprisonment up to one year.

It is also an offence to make a false statement or to knowingly give false information to an officer.

6

INCOME PROTECTION — THE WORKERS' COMPENSATION ACT

a. WHAT IS WORKERS' COMPENSATION?

Workers' compensation is a system of no-fault insurance that allows the employee to receive disability benefits without deduction for fault for personal injury or illness incurred during employment. An employee receives benefits until he or she is fit to return to work.

In return for the income protection this system affords, an employee may not sue the employer or other employees for damages. Such a system protects an employer from being bankrupted as a result of a large lawsuit. While the system restricts an employee's right to win large personal injury awards against his or her employer, employees are assured income while temporarily or permanently off work.

Administration and adjudication of workers' compensation are carried out by the Workers' Compensation Board.

b. WHO IS COVERED BY WORKERS' COMPENSATION?

Approximately 80% of employers in Alberta pay premium assessments to the Workers' Compensation Board. The Workers' Compensation Act covers all employers except those specifically excluded in the regulations. Industries excluded from the act include farming operations, finance houses, and professional offices. However, those employers excluded under the regulations may elect to voluntarily opt for protection. As well, some types of workers are excluded from coverage, including directors, partners, proprietors, and independent contractors. These people may elect to get coverage by voluntarily contributing premiums.

c. ELIGIBILITY

Full-time, part-time, seasonal, and casual workers in a "compulsory industry" are eligible for coverage, as are those covered by an employer who has voluntarily opted for protection. For an accident to be compensable, it must arise out of and occur in the course of employment in an industry to which the act applies. An accident includes a disabling or potentially disabling condition caused by an occupational disease (see section **d.** below).

A worker who suffers personal injury from an accident or occupational disease will receive compensation unless the serious and willful misconduct of the worker was the primary cause of the injury. However, if the worker is seriously disabled as a result of the accident, the board will pay compensation even if the injury was because of the worker's serious and willful misconduct.

d. OCCUPATIONAL DISEASE

Occupational diseases and conditions are listed in Schedule B of the regulations. Other diseases the board is satisfied were caused by particular conditions of employment are also considered occupational diseases.

Certain conditions of employment (also listed in Schedule B of the regulations) are deemed to have been causes of the listed diseases unless the contrary is proven. For example, significant occupational exposure to acid fumes is deemed to have caused erosion of incisor teeth. Significant occupational exposure to lead or lead compounds is deemed to have caused lead poisoning. Occupational exposure to airborne asbestos dust is deemed to have caused asbestosis, while occupational exposure to airborne silica dust (found in coal mining) is deemed to have caused silicosis.

e. CALCULATING BENEFITS

If an accident injures and disables a worker, the board pays periodic compensation to the worker based on the worker's net earnings. Net earnings are defined in the regulations as annual gross earnings less EI contributions, CPP contributions, and income tax likely payable.

Disability is classed as either permanent or temporary, and each case is defined as total or partial. Periodic payment of compensation for permanent total disability and temporary total disability is 90% of the worker's net earnings. Workers receive compensation for temporary total disability and temporary partial disability only so long as the disability lasts.

These injuries are considered permanent total disabilities:

- Total and permanent loss of sight in both eyes

- Loss of both feet above the ankle

- Loss of both hands at or above the wrist

- Loss of one hand and one foot

- Injury to spine resulting in paralysis of both legs, both arms, or one leg and one arm

- Injury to the central nervous system resulting in mental incompetence that renders the worker incapable of being gainfully employed

The board may reduce or suspend compensation to a worker if the worker acts in a way that endangers or delays his or her recovery, or refuses to undergo any medical aid that the board, based on independent medical advice, considers reasonably essential for his or her recovery.

In determining the degree of impairment of earning capacity, the board may consider as factors:

(a) the nature of the injury,

(b) the physical and mental fitness of the worker to continue in the employment in which he or she was injured, and

(c) the worker's ability to adapt to some other suitable employment.

f. EMPLOYER ASSESSMENT COSTS

Workers' compensation is financed entirely by the contribution of premiums by employers. The amount of contribution is based on the degree of hazard in the employer's industry and specific workplace history.

Employer premium rates are reviewed annually; premiums are based on the employer's assessable payroll at the rate established for the employer's industry.

g. CLAIMS

If a worker suffers personal injury in an accident, the worker must give notice to the employer as soon as possible. If the worker is likely to be disabled for more than one day after the accident, he or she must also give notice to the board as soon as possible. To make a claim, the employee must use the board's Worker's Report of Accident form. The report must include the full name and address of the worker and state in plain language the cause of the accident.

An employer who receives notice of an accident must record particulars of the accident in the accident record book. Particulars include:

(a) full name of the injured worker,

(b) date, time, and place of the accident,

(c) date when the accident was reported or the employer obtained knowledge of it,

(d) cause of the accident,

(e) description of the injury, and

(f) medical treatment given.

If the worker is likely to be disabled for more than one day after the accident, the employer has 72 hours to file an Employer's Report of Accident to the board. The employer is also required to notify the board once it has knowledge that the worker has returned to work or is able to return to work.

The doctor treating the injured worker has 48 hours to file an accident report to the board. The employee or the employee's dependant must file an application for compensation within one year from the accident causing injury. However, the board will waive this time limit if it is satisfied there are reasonable and justifiable grounds for the claim not being brought in the one-year period.

h. APPEAL

If an employee, dependant, or employer is not satisfied with the claims adjudicator's final settlement of a claim, he or she may request the claims services review committee appointed by the board to review the record. The written request must set out relevant particulars of the claim, the decision being appealed, and the grounds for the appeal. A request for review must be made one year from the decision. However, the chairperson of the committee may extend the one-year period if there are justifiable reasons.

The committee may require the worker to undergo, at the expense of the board, a medical examination by a physician not employed by the board. If the worker obstructs the medical examination in any way, his or her right to compensation is suspended until the examination is completed.

A worker, dependant, employer, or other interested party who is dissatisfied with the decision of the claims services review committee or the assessment committee may appeal the decision to the Appeals Commission. In considering an appeal, the commission must consider the record and give all interested parties an opportunity to be heard and to present any new or additional evidence. Unless the commission thinks there has been some justifiable delay, an appeal must be brought within one year from the date of the decision being appealed.

On review or on appeal, any interested party may be represented by a lawyer or any party the employee chooses. As well, the worker or dependant is entitled to be informed of any information the committee has that is contrary to the interests of that worker. This information must be given in enough detail that the party understands it.

i. DEATH BENEFITS

Workers' compensation provides death benefits when death is a direct result of injuries or illnesses incurred in the course of employment. This compensation replaces the rights of survivors to sue the employer for damages resulting from the accident or occupational disease.

The main recipient of the benefits is the spouse of the deceased employee.

If a worker dies as a result of an accident, leaving a dependent spouse, that spouse will receive a pension equal what the worker would have received had he or she lived and been permanently, totally disabled. Additional amounts are payable to the dependent spouse for dependent children (children under 18 years of age). Sometimes, the pension payable to a dependent spouse will be reduced if the spouse refuses vocational rehabilitation services. These services include physical, social, and psychological services, as well as job retraining or other rehabilitation services.

7

LABOUR RELATIONS AND THE LABOUR RELATIONS CODE

Organized labour presents a very different backdrop for the employee and employer relationship. How do trade unions achieve certification to bargain for specific groups of employees? What should employees do if they believe that the trade union has failed to represent their interests fairly in the course of collective bargaining? As well, employees' right to strike and employers' corresponding right to lock out pose powerful incentives for parties to bargain in good faith.

a. TO WHOM DOES THE CODE APPLY?

The Labour Relations Code applies to most unionized employees in the province. However, there are some major exceptions:

(a) Public service employees are governed by the Public Service Employee Relations Act.

(b) Employers and employees in farm or ranch labour, or domestic work are excluded.

(c) Employers and employees in industries falling under federal jurisdiction (e.g., airlines, railways, interprovincial trucking, shipping, and telecommunications) are excluded.

(d) Self-employed workers are not covered by the code.

(e) Some employees have their labour relations governed entirely or in part by special acts such as the

Colleges Act, the Technical Institutes Act, the Police Officers Collective Bargaining Act, and the School Act.

(f) Employees who, in the opinion of the board, exercise managerial functions or who are employed in a confidential capacity in matters relating to labour relations are excluded.

(g) Employees who are practising members of the medical, dental, architectural, engineering, and legal professions of Alberta are excluded.

b. PURPOSE OF THE CODE

The code guarantees employees the right to collectively bargain with their employers and establishes methods for employees to choose trade union representation. The code sets out how trade unions bargain with employers over terms and conditions of employment to arrive at a collective agreement. Once the collective agreement is in place, the code facilitates regulation of the activities of trade unions, employees, and employers.

c. THE ROLE OF THE LABOUR RELATIONS BOARD

The mandate of the Labour Relations Board is broad. Responsibilities of the board include:

- Administering the code and the Public Service Relations Act

- Making decisions about revoking trade union certification

- Conducting representation and proposal votes (see section **f.5.** below)

- Supervising strike and lockout votes

- Resolving disputes between unions and employers during the collective bargaining process

- Regulating picketing

- Hearing complaints of unfair labour practices and granting appropriate remedies

Hearings before the board are less formal than court trials. The board is not bound by rules of evidence. As a result, submitting evidence to the board is less complicated. Legal representation is optional, and sometimes parties before the board resolve the dispute themselves without the need for a board decision.

Board rulings are final, binding, and enforceable as a court order; there is no appeal of board decisions. However, if either party believes that the board exceeded its powers or interpreted the law in an unreasonable way, that party can apply for review to the Court of Queen's Bench within 30 days of the board's decision.

The board does not interpret the meaning or application of collective agreements; grievance arbitrators provide this function.

d. THE COLLECTIVE AGREEMENT

The collective agreement is the contract between the trade union and the employer and is binding on all employees in the bargaining unit, whether they are union members or not. (Bargaining units are discussed in greater detail below, in section **f.1.**)

Typical conditions of the agreement include those about wages, vacations, hours of work, seniority and promotions, layoff and recall or benefit plans, union security, as well as a grievance and arbitration provision.

e. TRADE UNIONS

The code defines a trade union as an organization of employees that has a written constitution, rules, or by-laws, and whose objects include the regulation of relations between employers and employees.

Trade unions represent a specific group of employees in negotiations with the employer. A trade union may be a local, provincial, national, or international union. It may be an independent organization that represents the employees of only one plant or business. Employees can either form their own trade union or join an existing one.

The collective agreement usually contains a provision about union security. There are five common types of arrangements for the trade union and employer to choose from.

(a) *The union shop:* An employee must become a union member within a specified time after being hired. The employee must pay union dues.

(b) *The closed shop:* A prospective employee must be a union member before the employer may hire him or her. The employee must pay union dues.

(c) *The agency shop, or the Rand formula:* While an employee does not need to be a union member, he or she must pay union dues.

(d) *Maintenance of membership:* A new member does not need to be a union member, but an existing union member must maintain union membership and continue paying union dues.

(e) *Dues check-off:* The employer deducts union dues upon written authorization from the employee.

If an employee cannot join the union or pay dues because of religious beliefs, he or she may give money equivalent to the union dues to a registered charity.

f. CERTIFICATION

A trade union may apply to the board to be certified as the bargaining agent for employees in a unit the trade union

considers appropriate for collective bargaining (see section
f.1 below).

A trade union's application for certification must include
evidence of 40% support of the trade union by the employees
in the unit applied for. This evidence can be membership lists,
application for membership cards, a combination of the two,
or petitions.

Membership applications must have been made less than
90 days before the date of the certification application. Appli-
cants for membership must pay their own $2 membership
fee; loans from a union organizer disqualifies the card. Inclu-
sion of invalid cards may cause the board to question the
merit of the entire certification application.

Petition evidence is a petition signed by each person
supporting the application. The union must choose support by petition evidence or membership evidence, as petition evidence cannot be combined with membership
evidence.

1. What is an appropriate bargaining unit?

Before it grants certification, the board must be satisfied
that the unit the trade union has applied for is appropriate.
For industries other than hospitals, nursing homes, community health, firefighting, and construction, the board
decides on the appropriate bargaining unit on a case-by-
case basis.

The board has a wide discretion in deciding appropriate
units. An appropriate bargaining unit is a group of employees that makes "labour relations sense" to group together for
collective bargaining. The board may certify more than one
unit. If the board finds that a unit applied for is inappropriate,
it may change the unit to one that is appropriate. This change
can be made only if there is an appropriate unit reasonably
similar to the one applied for.

(a) Factors the board considers

The board considers certain factors, including those listed below, when deciding what units are appropriate.

(a) *Community of interest.* The board determines if employees have common interests, skills, and working conditions. If the employees have conflicting interests, the bargaining unit is inappropriate. The prospect of conflicting interests sometimes favours smaller units.

(b) *Bargaining history.* The board determines if the employer is already bargaining with more than one bargaining agent. If not, the board will not certify a small group of employees "carved out" from a larger unit unless there are compelling labour relation reasons to do so.

(c) *Nature of the employer's organization.* If the employer operates in several different locations that are not integrated, the board is more likely to find that a local unit is appropriate.

(d) *Viable bargaining structures.* As larger bargaining units tend to be more effective, the board is inclined to favour the larger bargaining unit so long as there are no conflicts of interest among employees in the unit.

(e) *Avoidance of fragmentation.* As multiple units make it more difficult and costly for the employer, excessive fragmentation of bargaining units is discouraged.

(f) *Agreement of the parties.* The board is inclined to favour a proposed unit to which both the employer and trade union agree, unless the board feels that it is inappropriate.

(b) Board policies on certification

The board has published a list of "rules of thumb" about appropriate bargaining units. Those rules include the following:

(a) The board will not usually certify separate units of full-time and part-time employees. Casual, part-time, and full-time employees are usually in the same unit.

(b) Barring conflicts of interest, all employees of an employer are an appropriate unit.

(c) Usually, the board will make separate units for office and plant employees.

(d) If certification of a proposed unit would leave a small portion of employees without a unit, the board is inclined to include the "tag end" employees in the proposed unit.

2. Timing of certification application

The timing of the application for certification varies, depending on the bargaining agents and collective agreements already in place.

(a) If there is no collective agreement or certification of a bargaining agent for any employees in the unit, a trade union may apply at any time to the board for certification.

(b) If there is a bargaining agent but no collective agreement, the trade union must wait ten months from the date of certification of that bargaining unit.

(c) If a collective agreement has been in force two years or less, no application can be made until two months before the end of the collective agreement.

(d) If a collective agreement has been in force more than two years, application can be made:

(i) in the 11th or 12th month of the 2nd or any subsequent year of the term, in which case the application must be made at least ten months before the end of the term of the collective agreement, or

(ii) in the 2nd month immediately preceding the end of the term.

(e) If a union previously lost or withdrew a certification application for the unit, it must wait 90 days from the time of the previous application or get board consent.

(f) If a union has been decertified, it must wait six months before applying for recertification.

During a strike or lockout, a trade union needs permission from the board to apply for certification.

3. Prohibitions on certification

If the board feels the trade union is dominated or influenced by an employer to the extent that the trade union is unfit to collectively bargain for the employees in the unit, certification will not be granted. As well, a trade union will not be certified if it can be shown that membership in the union resulted from picketing at the affected employees's place of employment.

4. Statutory freeze

Once an application for certification has been made, an employer is prohibited from altering the rates of pay or conditions of work except if following an established custom or practice or with consent of the union. This freeze lasts until the application is refused or until 30 days have elapsed from the date certification was granted. For example, in one case, the employer gave evidence showing that pay raises implemented after an application for certification reflected a long-range plan and were approved before the certification application. The board decided that no unfair labour practice had occurred.

5. Representation vote

Once application for certification is complete, the board conducts a representation vote to determine if a majority of employees in the bargaining unit favours certification. The vote is by secret ballot, and the majority of those employees who actually vote determines the outcome of the vote. Votes are usually held at the workplace.

6. Voluntary recognition

A trade union may approach the employer directly and ask the employer to voluntarily recognize the trade union by agreeing to bargain with the union. The employer and the trade union can then negotiate a collective agreement. Voluntary recognition is most common in the construction industry.

The employer can end a bargaining relationship based on voluntary recognition by giving six months' notice before the collective agreement expires. The union may then respond by applying for certification.

7. Sale or merger of a business

When a business or part of a business is sold, leased, transferred, or merged with another business or with part of another business, the union's bargaining rights may continue to bind the new employer. The union or the employer may apply to the board to determine whether any existing certification or collective agreement remains binding.

8. Decertification

An application to revoke bargaining rights may be made by the trade union, employees in the unit, the employer, or the former employer. A trade union may apply for revocation of bargaining rights any time there is no collective agreement.

Employees may apply to have bargaining rights revoked in a window of time similar to those for certification applications (described in section 2. above). The employees' application for revocation of bargaining rights must be supported by evidence in a form satisfactory to the board that at least 40% of the employees within the unit have indicated their support for the revocation. No application can be brought without the board's consent if a strike or lockout is in effect.

An employer or former employer may apply to have bargaining rights revoked only if the employer or former employer and the bargaining agent have not bargained collectively for three years —

(a) after the date of certification, if no collective agreement has been entered into affecting the employer or former employer and the bargaining agent, or

(b) after the first date fixed for the end of the collective agreement, if a collective agreement has been entered into affecting the employer or former employer and the trade union.

When certification is revoked, the employer is not required to bargain with the union. Any collective agreement in force at the time of revocation becomes void. As well, the trade union may not apply for certification, negotiate, or enter into a collective agreement for the same or substantially the same unit for six months from the date of revocation.

g. COLLECTIVE BARGAINING

The objective of collective bargaining is to create a collective agreement between the trade union and the employer. This agreement governs wages and benefits for the employees in the union for the term of the collective agreement.

Once a trade union has been certified as a bargaining agent for a unit of employees, notice to begin bargaining toward a collective agreement is given. If there is no existing agreement, one party gives notice to the other party to begin collective bargaining. If there is an agreement, notice to begin bargaining may be made between 60 and 120 days before the collective agreement expires, unless the collective agreement specifies a longer period. Both parties must begin to bargain within 30 days of notification to begin collective bargaining.

The Labour Relations Code requires the employer and the trade union to bargain in good faith and to make every reasonable effort to come to an agreement. If one party feels the other party is failing to bargain in good faith, that party may file a complaint with the board. The board may issue directives or conditions to ensure good-faith bargaining resumes. However, the board will not settle the terms of the agreement itself, as that is the purpose of collective bargaining.

Once bargaining begins, the code automatically extends the terms of a collective agreement that would otherwise expire. This is known as bridging. Bridging continues until a legal strike or lockout takes place, until bargaining rights are terminated, or until a new collective agreement is entered into.

The construction industry is governed by different provisions of the Labour Relations Code (Part 3). Guidelines can be obtained from the Labour Relations Board.

h. MEDIATION

If disputes arise between the parties while trying to arrive at a collective agreement, either party may request the director of Mediation Services to appoint a mediator. The mediator tries to bring about a settlement between the parties after hearing both sides of the dispute. A mediator may also be appointed by a Minister of Labour.

Once a mediator is appointed, there must be 14 days of formal mediation. No strike or lockout is permitted until a further 14-day cooling-off period has passed. The mediator may issue a report containing recommendations; these are binding only if both parties accept the report. If only one side accepts, that side can apply for the board to conduct a vote by secret ballot for the other party. If, as a result of the vote, both parties accept the recommendation, the recommendations form the new collective agreement. If the parties don't agree or if the vote fails, the parties may —

(a) continue negotiating;

(b) agree to submit the dispute to voluntary arbitration; or

(c) consider a strike or lockout, but not until after the 14-day cooling-off period or after a vote on the mediator's report.

i. VOLUNTARY ARBITRATION

The parties to a dispute arising from attempts to arrive at a collective agreement may agree in writing to ask the minister to refer the disputed matters to a voluntary arbitration board. The board mediates between the parties and makes all possible efforts to bring about a settlement.

If unable to do so within 20 days or a longer period agreed on by the parties or fixed by the minister, the board will make an award dealing with all matters in dispute. This decision is binding on the parties and will be included in the terms of the collective agreement.

j. DISPUTE INQUIRY BOARD

Before a strike or lockout, the minister may notify the parties to a dispute that a disputes inquiry board has been established. If the inquiry board is established before the start of a lawful strike or lockout, no strike or lockout may begin until ten days after the parties receive a copy of the inquiry board recommendations or until 72 hours after the parties have been notified of the results of a vote on the recommendations.

If a majority of those polled at the employer organization or a majority of those employees who voted accepts the recommendations, the recommendations are binding on the parties and form part of the collective agreement. If the recommendations are rejected, the strike or lockout may begin.

If the inquiry board is set up after a strike or lockout has begun, the strike or lockout will not be affected.

k. STRIKES AND LOCKOUTS

If no collective agreement has been arrived at after the mediation process and cooling-off period, or after rejection of recommendations from a disputes inquiry board, the parties have the option of taking strike or lockout action. Strikes or lockouts are meant to apply pressure on the opposing party to reach settlement. A strike is employee withdrawal of services; a lockout is action taken by the employer to prevent employees from working and earning wages.

Before calling a strike, the trade union must apply to the Labour Relations Board to have the board supervise the strike vote. Similarly, an employer must apply to the board for a supervised lockout vote. The strike vote determines if a majority of the voting employees is prepared to go on strike. Any strike or lockout must occur no more than 120 days after the vote.

Finally, before the strike or lockout can take place, the union or employer, as the case may be, must give notice to the other party of the time, date, and initial location of the intended action. Notice must also be given to the board and, if appropriate, to the mediator or disputes inquiry board involved.

An employee cannot be dismissed simply for being on strike. When the strike or lockout ends, the employee is entitled to ask to resume his or her employment. That employee is entitled to be reinstated in preference to any employee hired as a replacement during the dispute. However, an employee must ask for reinstatement as soon as the strike or lockout is over. An employer is not required to reinstate employees if it can prove that no jobs are available because of production cutbacks or market slowdowns.

1. When can employees legally strike?

Employees can legally strike so long as:

(a) no collective agreement is in force (a bridging agreement is not considered a collective agreement for this rule),

(b) the strike vote showed a majority of voting employees wanted to strike,

(c) declaration of the strike vote is filed with the board,

(d) the strike is not more than 120 days after the strike vote, and

(e) the mediator and other party are given 72 hours notice of the strike.

2. When can the employer hold a legal lockout?

An employer can legally lockout so long as:

(a) there is no collective agreement (a bridging agreement is not considered a collective agreement for this rule),

(b) the majority of the employers in the employer organization or a poll of a single employer shows support for the lockout,

(c) lockout vote results are filed with the board,

(d) not more than 120 days have passed since the lockout vote, and

(e) the mediator and other party are given 72 hours' notice of the strike.

3. Picketing

Picketing may occur during a lawful strike or lockout. The picketing is restricted to the employee's place of employment. Unlike some other provinces, Alberta does not allow secondary picketing — picketing somewhere other than the place of employment.

Picketing must not entail unlawful acts of violence or trespass. An employee may be dismissed for participating in unlawful picketing. The Labour Relations Board is primarily responsible for regulating picketing activities during a strike or lockout.

An employee legally on strike may attend the site of employment and try to persuade anyone not to:

(a) enter the employer's place of business,

(b) deal in products of the employer, or

(c) do business with the employer.

The board considers the following when regulating picketing:

(a) the degree to which those people picketing are directly interested,

(b) the degree of violence or likelihood of violence in the picketing,

(c) the desirability of restraining picketing so the conflict does not escalate, and

(d) the right to peaceful, free expression of opinion.

4. Maintenance of essential services

The code has special rules to resolve disputes in certain essential services. Parties providing essential services must submit unresolved bargaining disputes to a binding arbitration that replaces the option to strike or lock out. These rules always apply to hospital employees and firefighters. A similar system applies to police under the Police Officers Collective Bargaining Act and to public servants under the Public Service Employee Relations Act.

These rules also apply when cabinet declares a dispute to be a public emergency. Factors considered in determining if there is an emergency include whether:

(a) damage to health or property is being caused by the stop of operation of a sewage system, water system, gas system, or reduction in health services; or

(b) unreasonable hardship is being caused to people not parties to the dispute.

Once an order of emergency is made, the strike or lockout must end. The issues in dispute must then be resolved through a form of arbitration called a public emergency tribunal.

1. GRIEVANCE ARBITRATION

The code requires that every collective agreement contain a mechanism for settling differences arising from the interpretation, application, or operation of the collective agreement. The method used is usually a grievance procedure followed by a form of arbitration called *grievance arbitration*, or *rights arbitration*. Employee discharge and discipline cases, disputes about overtime, and disputes over benefit payments are types of cases handled by arbitration. If the parties do not include a grievance procedure condition in the collective agreement, the code reads one in.

The arbitrator's decision is binding. While an arbitration award cannot be appealed to the board, the court will review a decision that was allegedly beyond the arbitrator's powers or that involved unreasonable errors of law. However, any application for review must be filed within 30 days of the arbitrator's decision.

m. A UNION'S DUTY OF FAIR REPRESENTATION

The code imposes a duty of fair representation on trade unions. This provision is intended to ensure that trade unions treat employees fairly. Employees who feel their union has treated them unfairly may file a complaint with the board.

The Supreme Court of Canada has held that unions have a duty to exercise their discretion in employee grievance cases with good faith, objectivity, and honesty. At the same time, employees must follow the grievance procedures set out in the collective agreement. The employee is responsible for keeping his or her losses to a minimum. For example, if the employee is fired, he or she must take another job to mitigate losses.

One common area of employee complaint is a union's decision on whether to take a particular grievance to arbitration. This decision must be made without ill will, discrimination, or prejudice. If there is a breach of the duty of fair representation, the board may make a declaration, award damages, or extend the time limits of the grievance. The board reviews the conduct of the union but does not interfere with the union's decision on the merits of the grievance.

n. OFFENCES AND PENALTIES

Under the code, any trade union that causes an illegal strike is guilty of an offence and liable to a fine of up to $1 000 for each day of the strike. A trade union representative can be fined up to $10 000 personally for consenting to an illegal strike. An ordinary employee can be fined up to $1 000. A general penalty provision states that any person who violates the code or order of the board is liable to a fine of up to $10 000 for a company, and up to $5 000 for an individual.

APPENDIX
ADDRESSES AND TELEPHONE
NUMBERS

a. EMPLOYMENT STANDARDS OFFICES

CALGARY
Main Floor
Elveden Centre
717 - 7th Avenue S.W.
T2P 0Z5
Tel: (403) 297-4339
Fax: (403) 297-5483

EDMONTON
Main Floor
9940 - 106th Street
T5K 2N2
Tel: (403) 427-3731
Fax: (403) 427-8837

GRANDE PRAIRIE
Room 3101
Provincial Building
10320 - 99th Street
T8V 6J4
Tel: (403) 538-5253
Fax: (403) 538-5403

LETHBRIDGE
Room 377
Provincial Building
200 - 5th Avenue S.
T1J 4C7
Tel: (403) 381-5477
Fax: (403) 381 5425

MEDICINE HAT
Room 103
Provincial Building
346 - 3rd Street S.E.
T1A 0G7
Tel: (403) 529-3520
Fax: (403) 529-3632

RED DEER
2nd Floor
4920 - 51st Street
T4N 6K8
Tel: (403) 340 5153
Fax: (403) 340-5210

ST. PAUL
Room 407
Provincial Building
5025 - 49th Avenue
T0A 3A4
Tel: (403) 645-6360
Fax: (403) 645-6352

To be connected to any of these offices toll free, call 310-0000.

If you are deaf or have a hearing impairment and have an TDD/TDY unit, call 427-9999 in Edmonton. If you are outside of Edmonton, call toll free 1-800-232-7215.

b. ALBERTA HUMAN RIGHTS AND CITIZENSHIP COMMISSION OFFICES

NORTHERN REGIONAL OFFICE
1600 Standard Life Centre
10405 Jasper Avenue
Edmonton, AB T5J 4R7
Tel: (403) 427-7661
Fax: (403) 427-6013

SOUTHERN REGIONAL OFFICE
Suite 102
1333 - 8th Street S.W.
Calgary, AB T2R 1M6
Tel: (403) 297- 6571
Fax: (403) 297-6567

c. ALBERTA LABOUR OFFICES

1. Central region

RED DEER
5th Floor
4920 - 51st Street
T4N 6K8
Tel: (403) 340-5170
Fax: (403) 340-7035

2. North central region

EDMONTON
9321 - 48th Street
T6B 2R4
Tel: (403) 427-8848
Fax: (403) 422-9645

EDSON
Room 110
111 - 54th Street
T7E 1T2
Tel: (403) 738-8201
Fax: (403) 723-8220

VERMILLION
4071 - 52nd Street
T0B 4M0
Tel: (403) 853-8142
Fax: (403) 853-8206

3. **Northwest region**

GRANDE PRAIRIE
Room 3401
10320 - 99th Street
T8V 6J4
Tel: (403) 538-5249
Fax: (403) 538-8056

4. **Southern region**

CALGARY
2nd Floor
1021 - 10th Avenue S.W.
T2R 0B7
Tel: (403) 297-2222
Fax: (403) 297-7893

LETHBRIDGE
3rd Floor
220 - 4th Street S.
T1J 4J7
Tel: (403) 381-5522
Fax: (403) 381-5761

MEDICINE HAT
Room 103
346 - 3rd Street S.E.
T1A 0G7
Tel: (403) 529-3520
Fax: (403) 529-3632

d. WORKERS' COMPENSATION BOARD OFFICES

CALGARY

300 - 6th Avenue S.E.
T2G 0G5
Tel: (403) 297-6471
Fax: (403) 297-2227

Office Of The Appeal Advisor
602 - 1701 Centre Street N.
T2E 7Y2
Tel: (403) 297-6501
Fax: (403) 297-6550

EDMONTON

Claims Information
107 Street Building
9912 - 107th Street
P.O. Box 2415
T5J 2S5
Tel: (403) 427-1131
Fax: (403) 427-5863

WCB Millard Rehabilitation Centre
7123 - 119th Street
T6G 1V7
Tel: (403) 430-5000
Fax: (403) 437-4289

Office of the Appeals Advisor
5th Floor
10621 - 100th Avenue
T5J 0B3
Tel: (403) 498-8640
Fax: (403) 422-2888

GRANDE PRAIRIE
1022 - 102nd Avenue
T8V 0Z7
Tel: (403) 538-5421
Fax: (403) 538-5689

LETHBRIDGE
1st Floor
1 Chancery Court
220 - 4th Street S.
T1J 4J7
Tel: (403) 381-5339
Fax: (403) 381-5764

RED DEER
208 Centre 5010 Building
5010 - 43rd Street
T4N 6H2
Tel: (403) 340-5357
Fax: (403) 340-7786

The Workers' Compensation Board can be accessed toll free by calling the provincial government's RITE lines at 310-0000.

e. LABOUR RELATIONS BOARD OFFICES

CALGARY
Labour Relations Board
Deerfoot Junction, Tower 3
Suite 308
1212 - 31st Avenue N.E.
T2E 7S8
Tel: (403) 297-2338
Fax: (403) 297-5884

EDMONTON
Labour Relations Board
Suite 503
10808 - 99th Avenue
T5K 0G5
Tel: (403) 427-8547
Fax: (403) 422-0970

ANOTHER BUSINESS TITLE FROM SELF-COUNSEL

A SMALL BUSINESS GUIDE TO EMPLOYEE SELECTION
Finding, interviewing, and hiring the right people
Lin Grensing
$7.95

This book offers employers practical information on how to success-fully select productive employees. It includes sample advertisements, application forms, suggested interview questions, and role-play exercises for the interviewer/applicant exchange.

Some of the questions answered are:

- What do I need to know before I advertise for the new position?

- How do I screen resumes effectively?

- What questions should I ask the candidates during the interview?

- Do I have to worry about human rights laws when I am hiring?

- What if an employee has AIDS?

- What should I consider before introducing a drug-testing plan at my company?

- What is the best way to make a new employee feel comfortable? How can top employees be encouraged to stay?

ORDER FORM

All prices are subject to change without notice. Books are available in book, department, and stationery stores. If you cannot buy the book through a store, please use this order form. (Please print)

Name_____

Address_____

_____

Charge to: ❑ Visa   ❑ MasterCard

Account Number_____

Validation Date_____Expiry Date_____

Signature_____

YES, please send me:

_____ **A Small Business Guide to Employee Selection** $7.95

Please add $3.00 for postage and handling.
Please add 7% GST to your order.

❑   **Check here for a free catalogue.**

Please send your order to:

Self-Counsel Press
1481 Charlotte Road
North Vancouver, BC
V7J 1H1

Visit our Internet Web Site at:
http://www.self-counsel.com